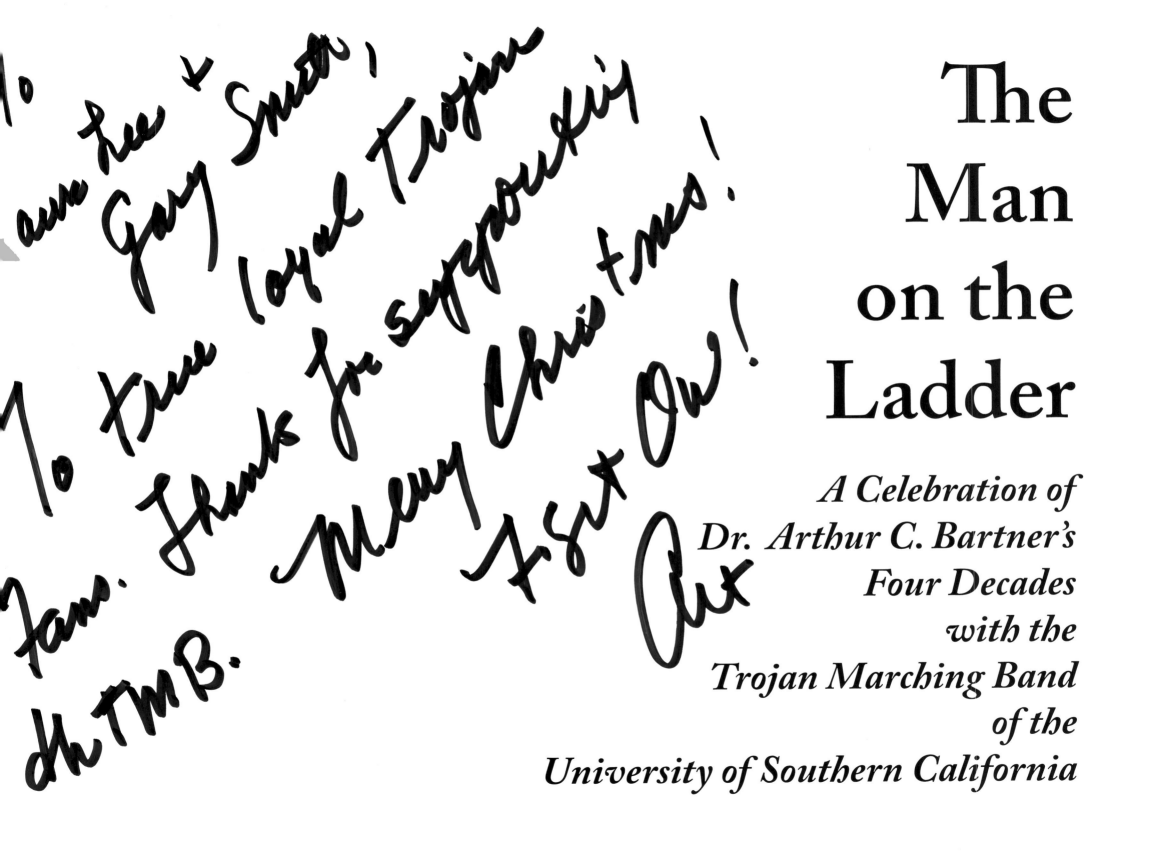

The Man on the Ladder

A Celebration of
Dr. Arthur C. Bartner's
Four Decades
with the
Trojan Marching Band
of the
University of Southern California

Written and designed by Keith H. Walker and Robert W. Jensen

Jensen & Walker, Inc.
Los Angeles, California

Research by Brett Padelford

©2010 University of Southern California - Trojan Marching Band

Produced and distributed by Figueroa Press
840 Childs Way, Los Angeles, CA 90089

Printed in the USA by Wright Color Graphics, Sun Valley, California

Library of Congress Control Number 2010925735

First Printing: April 2010

Made possible by a grant from Craig and Susan Caldwell

A letter from Pete Carroll, who coached the Trojan Football Team from 2001 through 2009, chalking up two national titles, seven Pac-Ten Championships, seven BCS bowls, three Heisman Trophy winners and 97 wins in 116 games:

When Dr. Art Bartner first started at USC four decades ago, legend has it that renowned assistant football coach Marv Goux came up, grabbed him by the neck and had a few words for him. "This band should be much better," Goux sternly told Bartner. The Trojan Marching Band wasn't anything special in 1970, just another collegiate ensemble that showed up on game days.

Similarly, when I first started at USC a decade ago, Coach Goux came up to me and had some words to pass along. "This football team should be much better," he told me in a stern voice. In 2000, the Trojans were coming off a losing season for just the third time in 40 years.

Looks like Coach Goux was right on both accounts — and especially for Dr. Bartner. Dr. Bartner has turned an average band into one of the world's most renowned. The Trojan Marching Band has produced platinum albums with famous artists. They have performed at every football game since 1987. They have played in movies, during Hollywood awards shows and all over TV. The list literally goes on and on.

But perhaps most importantly, the Trojan Marching Band has revolutionized USC school spirit during Dr. Bartner's 40 years at the university. The Trojan Marching Band is the magnetic force that brings the Trojan Family together, unifying us all with the battle cries, the stabbing of midfield, the rendition of "Tusk," the shiny gold helmets, the unwavering shouts of "Fight On!" and, of course, those chants about someone's "Big Balls."

What Dr. Bartner has done is simply incredible. He has taken something and turned it into a constant winner that just screams of success and achievement and greatness. He has set an example for how all of us should live our lives — you become the best by maximizing your opportunities in whatever is in front of you. And that is exactly what Dr. Bartner has become — the best. But how has he done it? And — this is the coolest part — how does he continue to do it year after year?

For one, it's hard work. The work ethic Dr. Bartner and his hundreds and thousands of band members have displayed over the years has developed them into the extraordinary band they are today. There's a saying around our program that "practice is everything." The Trojan Marching Band sure lives that, and it shows with spectacular performances and unending displays of school spirit.

Another thing that stands out is the band's style. The slick shades, shiny helmets and heroic tunes exude pure class, something all USC alumni and fans are proud of. And the best part is that it's class with humility. The band isn't arrogant or cocky — they are who they are, and it's awesome. And all that flows from Dr. Bartner, who has done it all with class, humility and style.

Lastly, you've got to applaud the Trojan Marching Band's consistency. No matter when you see them — 6 a.m. during Fall Camp or 11 p.m. after a game — they're always full of energy, looking sharp and playing well. They're everywhere, too — at games, practices, weddings, on TV. It's awesome, and a reflection of how much the band is loved and appreciated by all.

It's one thing to do something well, but it's quite another to do something well day after day after day. And that's exactly what Dr. Bartner and the Trojan Marching Band have done. They've achieved consistent excellence, something for which we all should be always striving.

It's funny, because a lot of the principles that Dr. Bartner has used to become great and develop a great program are what we use in our football program. Dr. Bartner and his band members show the same effort and enthusiasm that we show on the football field and in the film room day-in and day-out. The band's energy fuels our fans and university in tremendous ways, and it's one of the most important traditions of this fine institution.

Bottom line, thank you, Dr. Bartner for all you've done and been for USC in your 40 years. Coach Goux would be proud. We all are.

Photos on pages 6-7 and 8-9:

These photos illustrate what, Dr. Bartner describes in his own words as, "My favorite moment after the Trojans win a game, when the team and band face each other, the band playing **Conquest!**, *and all the students, alumni and faculty (including Coach Carroll in the first photo) have their hands in the air making the Victory sign with their fingers—it's truly an emotional climax evoking the Trojan family."*

Right:

Dr. Arthur C. Bartner leading the Trojan Marching Band.

table of contents

Left and Opposite:

The Trojan Marching Band performs prior to the USC-UCLA game at the Rose Bowl in December 2008. Dr. Bartner proudly explained, "I've been to the Rose Bowl and marched in the Rose Parade 16 times with USC winning 12 of those games. Only Michigan has more appearances than that of all the other 20 Big Ten and Pac-10 schools."

Photo on pages 12-13:

The Trojan Marching Band assembles on the field before a game with Notre Dame at South Bend, Indiana.

Conquest! *rally on campus before the 2009 UCLA-USC football game.*

The Yell Leaders and Song Girls precede the football team onto the field before the game.

Opposite:
A B-2 stealth bomber did a flyover as the Trojan Marching Band played the national anthem before the Rose Bowl, January 1, 2009. In front of a crowd of 93,293, USC defeated Penn State 38-24. This was the fourth consecutive Rose Bowl and the third win in a row for USC. This shot was taken from a single-engine Cessna T206 at 4,500 feet.

Left:
Mark Sanchez takes the sword on the ladder as the band plays Conquest! *after the Trojans defeated Penn State, which, as it turned out, was his last game as a Trojan.*

Left:
The Trojan Marching Band joins with the Los Angeles Philharmonic Orchestra for Tchaikovsky's 1812 Overture *at the Hollywood Bowl.*

Right:
Dr. Bartner described, what he called his first memorable moment in his career at USC, "It was 1973 during my third year when the team went to the Rose Bowl for the first time since I had become band director. Diana Ross, who was nominated for an Academy Award for Lady Sings the Blues, *was scheduled to sing with the band at halftime, performing* Our Love is Here To Stay. *I sat through the first half wondering if she was going to show up. Sure enough, she arrived by helicopter outside the stadium during the first quarter. And, it happened. To top things off, John McKay, one of USC's great coaches led the team to a 42-17 victory over Ohio State."*

In December of 1979, the Trojan Marching Band attained "rock star" status for the first time with their five sold out performances at the Forum with Fleetwood Mac. Dr. Bartner remembered, "During the rock band's performance of Tusk, *a curtain opened revealing the Trojan Marching Band. The crowd went wild. Band members not only signed autographs for fans after the concert, but also received rave reviews from the crowd and press alike."*

Left:
The Trojan Marching Band renewed its rock star credentials in May of 1997 in a reunion with Fleetwood Mac in a live concert at the Burbank Studios of Warner Brothers, playing two charts — Tusk *and* Don't Stop Thinking About Tomorrow *which was the theme song of the Clinton campaign. A CD and DVD of the concert was published as* The Dance, *selling five million copies, more than double what* Tusk *sold in 1979, making this the Trojan Marching Band's second platinum album.*

At the 2009 Grammy Awards, Thom Yorke and Jonny Greenwood were joined by the Trojan Marching Band for a performance of 15 Step, *the lead track from the Radiohead's* In Rainbows *album.*

In the Trojan Marching Band's first appearance on the Grammy Awards in 2004, they backed up André 3000 of the hip-hop megagroup Outkast for the finale at the Staples Center, performing their number one hit, Hey Ya.

Opposite:
The 48th Annual Academy Awards were presented on
March 29, 1976 in the Dorothy Chandler Pavilion of
the Music Center in Los Angeles. On that occasion,
the Trojan Marching Band truly attained the status
of "Hollywood's Band," and Dr. Bartner said, "It was
the first Hollywood home run of my career." He had
become friends with Hank Ehrlich, who at the time
was Paramount's Publicity Director, and that year,
Paramount was hosting the Academy Awards. Bartner
describes what happened: "Hank was a big Trojan
fan so he was instrumental in getting Howard Koch,
the producer of the awards show, to invite the band
to perform in the finale. This was where I first met
composer John Williams who was the musical director of
the show. Elizabeth Taylor and Gene Kelly introduced
the band. We played America the Beautiful. *I was*
conducting from the side of the stage. The drum line
came up on a riser in front of all the stars who had won
awards, and the band literally filled the house, coming in
from every entrance on the stage, down the aisles—
it was fantastic!"

Opposite:
Two weeks after the Trojan Marching Band's crowd pleasing performance at the Grammys, fifty members of the band in top hats and tuxedos formed an all-male drum line at the 81st Annual Academy Awards in February of 2009 at the Kodak Theatre in Hollywood. The percussionists accompanied Hugh Jackman and Beyoncé (center stage) and Vanessa Hudgens, Zac Efron and Amanda Seyfried in a medley featuring Top Hat, Mamma Mia, *and several other Broadway classics. The drum line exited the stage through a star-studded crowd that included Angelina Jolie and Brad Pitt, who leaned forward applauding and commenting "great show."*

Left:

On the football field at Pepperdine University in July 1984, Dr. Arthur C. Bartner directed a rehearsal of the Olympic All American College Marching Band made up of 800 students from colleges from every state in the United States. He recalled, "We rehearsed from 8:30 in the morning 'til 10 at night. Some of those night rehearsals were just marvelous—I can remember the trumpets did Maria *from* West Side Story, *and it was fabulous."*

Below:

Dr. Arthur C. Bartner directed the All American College Marching Band at the opening ceremony of the 1984 Olympics in the Coliseum. He described the evening's end, "As the band boarded the buses after the opening, I walked alongside each bus, high-fiving these great kids as they leaned out of the windows. It was as if they had won gold medals, they knew they'd been a part of history—a great moment in front of the world."

Above:
At the opening of the 1984 Olympics, a card stunt showing the flags of all the participating countries was a part of the celebration.

Left:
The mass band at the opening of the 1984 Olympics featuring the percussion section performing Sing, Sing, Sing.

Left:
David Wolper, producer of the opening ceremony for the 1984 Olympics in Los Angeles, points to a model of the Coliseum. (left to right) Tommy Walker, Jack Elliott, David Wolper, Dr. Arthur C. Bartner, John Williams.

A letter from David Wolper

Forty Years of WOW!

In 1984, I was the producer of the Opening and Closing Ceremonies of the Los Angeles Olympic Games. The theme of the opening ceremonies was a salute to American music and, given the giant stadium, I felt we had to have an American tradition, the marching band.

As a USC alumnus, Dr. Arthur C. Bartner immediately came to mind. At my first meeting with him, I explained what I wanted and he came up with the perfect concept right away, saying, "Let's have one of the biggest and best marching bands ever. How about 800 of the best musicians from every university in the country? Can you imagine what a sound that would be?" I knew he was probably the only person who could pull it off so I crossed my fingers behind my back and said, "Let's do it."

The first time I heard the 800 playing was at a rehearsal on the Coliseum floor. As they started to march and play every workman in the stands stopped and just watched in awe. I got goosebumps it was so powerful. I rushed down onto the field, hugged Art and told him, "You did it, by God, you did it!" It was, as expected, a huge hit at the Olympics.

I was asked to produce the four day celebration for the 100th Anniversary of the Statue of Liberty. Guess who I call to put together the marching band for that event? He again brought the best from the country. I went to one of the rehearsals and I've never seen such respect from a band for their leader. They went through a number and Art told them it wasn't very good – Art was a tough task master, he wanted perfection. He led them through a redo for me, and it was terrific. I've never seen a bunch of prouder young men and women. They knew he was right. They proved it by being a great success at the four-day celebration.

Every member of the Trojan Marching Band over the past forty years is proud to have been a part of it. They walk tall because of the great leadership of my friend, Dr. Arthur C. Bartner.

The opening ceremonies of the XXIII Olympiad Games at the Los Angeles Coliseum in 1984. Dr. Bartner formed a mass band composed of college students from every state. In this photo, they form the outline of the United States, with performers from the finale of the Music of America *show within.*

Opposite:
Dr. Arthur C. Bartner led the All American College Marching Band, comprised of band members from all over the country, including the Trojan Marching Band drum line and Silks, at the Liberty Weekend opening ceremony held on Governor's Island in New York celebrating the re-dedication of the Statue of Liberty on July 3, 1986. As already mentioned, David Wolper was the producer and Tommy Walker was the director. Walker was place kicker for the Trojans in the late forties, as well as drum major, and later band director for USC. He went on to become vice president of entertainment at Disneyland in Anaheim, California. That same weekend, the drum line performed for President Reagan on an aircraft carrier in New York Harbor.

The opening of the
Nixon Library in Yorba
Linda, California was
interpreted in a painting
(opposite) by Robert W.
Jensen. Dr. Bartner
explained how the
Trojan Marching Band
happened to be there for
the opening: "As you
probably know, President
Nixon's wife, Pat, was
a graduate of USC so it
was a natural association
for us. We had played
for them on several
occasions, including at
their summer home in
San Clemente. President
Nixon, at one event,
went up and down the
lines, shaking hands with
all the band members."

Left:
Dr. Bartner proudly declared, "We've
played for six presidents; for President
Reagan's inauguration in Washington, D.C.
I remember it was so cold, they canceled
the parade so we performed in the Capital
Center. And when he returned to Los
Angeles, we performed at the airport. A
photo of him wearing one of our Trojan
Band helmets (left) made all the wire
services and appeared in papers all over
the country. Of course, we've played out
in the Valley at his library too.   We played
for President Bush, (senior) when he
came to Los Angeles. Another president
we performed for was Gerald Ford when
he visited our campus.   Since he was a
University of Michigan graduate, and so
was I, it meant something special to me."

Left:
Pregame concert outside the Rose Bowl at the USC–UCLA game in December 2008.

Right:
Trojan mascot Traveler performs with the band at every game to the accompaniment of Conquest! *Dr. Bartner explained, "The horse appeared as a mascot when Bob Jani and Ed Tannenbaum suggested it in 1951. Famed Hollywood composer Alfred Newman composed the music* Conquest! *which the band plays when the horse is ridden after every USC touchdown. Bob Jani who became USC's director of special events was also a band alumnus."*

The Song Girls dance to the music of the Trojan Marching Band in Notre Dame Stadium.

A letter from Ann Bothwell

Fond Memories or How Friendships Are Born

My late husband, Lindley, was very much involved with both Yell Leaders, and the Song Girls (having dreamed them up in 1968). It was his practice to be on the sidelines before games, during halftime, to confer with the squads, etc. Our seats were (and still are) in the 5th row, on the 50 yard line, which put Art's ladder right in front of us.

When Art was very new to USC (1970), and at one of his very early games, during one of his half-times on the field, and when Art was between musical numbers, Lindley went up to him and tried to say, or ask him something. Major mistake. Art all but yelled (I think I must have heard him), and said "DON'T EVER TALK TO ME WHEN I AM CONDUCTING."

I have no recollection of what Lindley may have responded, but when he came back to his seat, looking very sheepish, and told me what had just happened, he thought that was that — he and Art would probably never speak to each other.

Of course it didn't take too long before they became the best of friends. While not always agreeing, their mutual intentions were always in accord — they both wanted whatever was best for the band, the girls and THE SHOW.

When Lindley was undergoing some surgical procedures, Art took time away from a very busy schedule to visit him in the hospital. One afternoon when I walked in, there were the two of them, Art in a chair, Lindley in bed, both of them sound asleep with an empty box which had contained homemade Danish cookies left by a friend the night before.

How's that for friendship?

Right:
The band
and the
Song Girls
perform before
the premiere of
High School
Musical 3
at USC's
Galen Center.

A letter from Tony Fox
Associate Director/Arranger

Above:
Tony Fox and Dr. Bartner
conferring during a game at the
Coliseum.

It's hard to believe that Art and I have been together close to 40 years but it's true! I can still remember the first time we met and discussed the possibility of me arranging for the USC Band. As they say in Hollywood: the rest is history. It was a match for the ages.

It began in 1971, we were both just beginning our careers, Art as a college band director and I as an arranger. I remember our first Band Camp together. At the time we were busy making things work; there was a lot of rebuilding to do in all areas of the program. We didn't think about the future, fame or notoriety; we just wanted the guys to behave, march and play as a unit. Little did we know we were witnessing the birth of one of college football's greatest institutions.

So many great memories, bowl games and special events: from the 1973 Rose Bowl halftime show featuring Diana Ross to the present; Super Bowls, the 1984 Olympics, the Rededication of The Statue of Liberty, the opening of Epcot and Euro Disney, Academy Awards ceremonies, Stars on the Hollywood Walk of Fame, movies, TV shows, commercials, trips around the world, all the wonderful guest artists that have performed for us too numerous to name and who could ever forget *Tusk.* Wow, what a ride we've had!

We have great mutual admiration and respect for each other; we have always been honest with each other; he knows my strengths and weaknesses and I know his. He is the Captain and I the Executive Officer of this ship called the Trojan Band. You could say we are the dream team of collegiate bands.

That meeting in 1971 set into motion so much more than either of us could have ever imagined. I am very proud to say I have worked side by side with Art, for he is the best at what he does and that has made me a better arranger.

Above:
USC Coach Larry Smith conducts the Trojan Marching Band. It was in the late eighties when coach Smith took the USC team to Michigan and was beaten so badly that a major policy change came about. When he came back, he made the statement that he would never go on the road again without the Trojan Marching Band. "That's a perfect example," says Bartner, "of how much the band had come to mean to the football team in terms of spirit. Since that time, we have some portion of the band at every away game."

Left:
Entering the Coliseum, marching down the Peristyle steps. The Silks holding flags line the steps on both sides.

Opposite:
Famed filmmaker George Lucas, USC Alumnus, with Dr. Bartner at a game against Washington State in October of 2005. Lucas stated: "Dr. Arthur Bartner has done a fantastic job directing the Trojan Marching Band. There is nothing like watching The Spirit of Troy march together in perfect lock-step while playing the beloved USC Fight Song. Congratulations to Dr. Bartner for 40 years of inspiring Trojans everywhere through his leadership."

Above:
The Trojan Marching Band plays at a pep rally before the Orange Bowl in Florida in 2003 where USC beat the Hawkeyes of the University of Iowa 38-17.

Right:
The tuba section plays a Happy Birthday *salute for one of their members.*

In 1973, the Trojan Marching Band made its first trip to a Notre Dame game wearing uniforms designed by Disney that include what everyone called "moon boots and brush helmets." The band played the Edgar Winter group hit, Frankenstein, *at half time shocking the stadium audience since they had never heard a rock chart number from a marching band before—nevertheless giving the band a three-minute standing ovation.*

Above and right: More views of the early uniforms designed by Disney with the band playing from the stands.

Opposite:
A pregame entrance of the band at the Coliseum in 1986 wearing a variation of the uniform with the super-shiny helmets that required most of the band to start wearing sun glasses. Within a short time, all of the band members added sun glasses to the ensemble which became a USC Trojan Marching Band trademark.

Overleaf, pages 54-55:
At the Coliseum, the band is playing Fight On!
into the spellout of USC on the field.

Opposite:
Super Bowl XXIV 1990, the Broncos vs. the 49ers at the
New Orleans Superdome. Dr. Arthur C. Bartner directed
a mass band comprised of students from colleges in the
area. The theme of the extravaganza was "A Salute to
New Orleans." The finale featured a massive riverboat
replica that "docked" at the 50 yard line with jazz legends
Pete Fountain and Al Hirt playing clarinet and trumpet
respectively from the upper deck.

This was just one of four Super Bowls that Dr. Bartner
worked on over a seven year period. In 1987, he directed
the USC Trojan Marching Band in a performance with
Mickey Rooney for Super Bowl XXI in the Rose Bowl in
Pasadena. In 1988, for Super Bowl XXII in Jack Murphy
Stadium in San Diego, it was another mass band of college
students from Southern California. And in 1993,
Super Bowl XXVII was again at the Rose Bowl,
with Michael Jackson.

Another memorable moment for Dr. Bartner at Jack
Murphy Stadium was when he had to leap from his ladder
to tackle one of two San Diego fans who were attempting
to disrupt the halftime performance by attacking drum
major Bijon Watson. The Los Angeles Times *reported: "If*
the USC defense had been able to tackle San Diego State's
Marshall Faulk as well as Bartner corralled one of two
half-time interlopers, the Trojans might have won instead
of hanging on for a 31–31 tie."

Opposite:
After the triumph of the Summer Olympic Games, Dr. Bartner presented an Olympic themed half-time Salute to America at the Rose Bowl Game on January 1, 1985. The Trojan Marching Band performed God Bless America *as they formed a star shape surrounding a massive inflatable Statue of Liberty that rose from the center of the field. Some 5,000 red, white and blue balloons were released as the statue was inflated. The Tommy Walker — inspired spectacle had the crowd cheering and the opposing football teams too mesmerized to warm up for the second half of the game. USC defeated the Ohio State Buckeyes 20-17.*

Opposite:
In the past, USC invited all of
the high school bands in the area
to participate in a mass band
at the Coliseum with
Dr. Arthur C. Bartner directing.
Celebrities have also joined in to
guest conduct, including
Steve Allen, Danny Kaye,
Michael Kamen, Elmer Bernstein,
and Richard Sherman.

Left:
Comedian Danny Kaye
guest conducted the
Trojan Marching Band at
the Homecoming game
in the Coliseum in 1985.

This Page and Opposite: In 2005, the Trojan Marching Band went to the Orange Bowl in support of the team who beat Oklahoma 55-19. These two photos show the pep rally in Miami Beach the day before the game.

Left:
Celebrating Dr. Arthur C. Bartner's 25th Anniversary with the Trojan Marching Band at the Coliseum culminated with fireworks over the peristyle. The most moving moment of the evening was a speech by assistant coach Marv Goux, who was a mentor to Dr. Bartner. The coach brought back memories of the 70's Friday afternoon jock rallies, and ended with the words, "I love you, Art." Other performers included Mick Fleetwood, Louis Bellson, Bill Conti and Dale Kristien. Another famous USC Alumnus, LeVar Burton was master of ceremonies.

Opposite:
The drum major stabs the 50 yard line at the start of the Trojan Marching Band's pre-game show. This was the 2009 Rose Bowl game which saw USC beat Penn State 38-24.

Opposite:
The Trojan Marching Band
playing a concert at Navy Pier
with the Chicago skyline in the
background. A tradition that
began in 1973, when USC plays
Notre Dame, the band travels on
Thursday, plays a concert for the
citizens of Chicago on Friday,
a pep rally that night, then the
game on Saturday. This concert
on Navy Pier was in 2007. The
concerts have also been given in
Daley Plaza.

Opposite Page:
In a special throw back to the
ultimate collegiate performance,
the USC Trojan Marching Band
performed on television with
Macy's Stars of Dance *doing KC*
and the Sunshine Band's Get Down
Tonight, *along with a special dance*
routine choreographed by Stomp
the Yard *choreographer Chuck*
Maldonado and performer Jimmy
R.O. Smith, on Dancing with the
Stars *in September 2009.*

Above:
Some 31.7 million viewers in the United States see the Trojan
Marching Band on the Season 7 Finale of American Idol **at the Nokia**
Theater in Los Angeles in 2008.

The Trojan Marching Band marches down field at the beginning of halftime.

Another tradition established by the band—whenever a touchdown is made by USC, Tommy Trojan rides Traveler around the field to accompaniment of the band playing Conquest!

A letter from John Williams

If we ask ourselves which educator, over the past 40 years, has consistently and skillfully put more talented feet on the ground, aimed more hearts and minds in the right direction, and synchronized the hands, embouchures and fingers of thousands of young people...the answer has to be Art Bartner.

Over these same 40 years I've watched Art display a combination of enviable gifts, among them an effusive energy, boundless enthusiasm and the rare ability to combine fun and rigorous discipline in the same package. It's a formula that, when applied to sound, makes music, and when applied to life, creates success...and it's a formula that Art Bartner lives his life by.

He lives a legacy of joyous music making and fine leadership and over these many years I've often wondered how many millions of people have been roused to the Trojan cause by his spirited performances of the "Conquest March." His tenure is sure to be remembered as a very bright chapter in the history of USC.

Art Bartner has earned his place in the pantheon of outstanding men and women who have served this great institution and it's a joy to celebrate the life and work of this extraordinary man.

Left:
In the 2004 Rose Bowl Game, the band performed John Williams' special arrangement of The Star Spangled Banner *under his direction in a combined performance with the Michigan Band during pregame festivities. Combine this with a card stunt that filled the Rose Bowl, and B-2 Stealth Bomber flyover, it became a truly memorable event. The Trojans beat the Wolverines 28-14 and win their first national championship since 1978.*

Above:
Composer John Williams with Dr. Bartner.

The trombone section at the UCLA-USC game of 2008.

A letter from Dennis R. Packer
Voice of The Spirit of Troy

This is my 21st season as a member and friend of the Trojan Marching Band. I do not play an instrument, wear a uniform, march during pre-game or half-time, march in parades, serve as a teaching assistant, compose music or work with the prop crew.

Since 1988, I have been the voice of The Spirit of Troy, writing and announcing pre-game and half-time shows for home games and the games played at Cal, Stanford, Notre Dame and bowl games, and special appearances by the band at band competitions throughout the Southland.

In addition, since 1990, I have been one of only a handful of announcers around the country, to be the stadium announcer and the band announcer. During these memorable years, my wife Judy and I have been privileged to have become close friends of Dr. Bartner and his wife Barbara, their friends Jerry and Diane, and each of their family members. His high regard for family, excellence in music performance and unwavering support of Trojan athletics, has shown through in the development of The Spirit of Troy into the greatest collegiate marching band in the universe.

Thank you, Dr. Bartner, for your 40 years of dedication, perseverance and excellence, and for allowing me to be a part of the Trojan Marching Band.

A letter from Keith Jackson
ABC Sports 1966-2006

My time spent covering college football must include more than a hundred games involving the Southern California Trojans and I really don't remember one that didn't include the Trojan Marching Band. It may be hard to believe but I actually did some Trojan games before Art Bartner arrived at USC.

But let me hasten to say that his presence, his energy, his persona and his genius were obvious immediately and remain so. And we are all richer for it.

Doctor Art Bartner ....you're a "Dandy" ...and this ole sports announcer is one of your biggest fans!

In 1990, Dr. Bartner was called upon to create a mass band from all the colleges in the Northwest for the Goodwill Games held in Seattle, Washington.

A mass band formation at Dodger Stadium in Los Angeles for the opening ceremonies of the U.S. Olympic Festival in 1991. Dr. Bartner formed and directed the band comprised of high school students from all over Los Angeles.

77

Acting as drum major, Dr. Bartner leads a mass band he created from East Coast college musicians in a parade in Philadelphia in 1987 commemorating the 200th Anniversary of the United States Constitution.

In 1992, Japan beckoned for Dr. Bartner to create a 20-piece band for the opening of the recreation of a Dutch Royal Family residence called Huis Ten Bosch, in Nagasaki.

Dr. Bartner leading his first All American College Band at Walt Disney World in Florida in 1974. The program was 11 weeks, actually performing in the park for 9 weeks. Out of an 8 hour day, they had clinics from the best jazz musicians in the United States. The band members were from colleges all over the country.

"From 20 musicians in 1974, " Dr. Bartner explained, *"we went to 400 musicians for the opening of Epcot in 1982. There were four students from a hundred colleges and universities. We worked together for a week culminating in the opening ceremony when it rained on our first performance. The band split into two groups marching around the lake from opposite directions and coming together. Then a concert the next day—it's a miracle the uniforms dried over night. The Disney career lasted for 28 years. I retired in 2005, but remained as a consultant. It all began with a USC Alumnus, Bob Jani, hiring me. He directed special events at USC and was truly a creative genius with unbelievable showbiz instincts. I count him as one of my most important mentors. From the beginning in 1974, I went on to do the 25th Anniversary of Walt Disney World, and the 50th of Disneyland, and all of these experiences opened doors for special events all over the country and the world. One was the dedication of a shopping center for the Rouse Company in St. Louis involving a 5,000-member high school mass band, the largest band I've ever conducted. Just getting them to play one note together was thrilling. "*

Left:
The mass band, created by and under the direction of Dr. Bartner, composed of American high school musicians from all over the country, march down the main street of Euro Disney, near Paris on opening day in 1992—a far cry from the tiny band and meager resources of 1974 when he began at Walt Disney World in Florida.

Opposite:
Dr. Bartner's All American College Marching Band, comprised of students from colleges all over the nation, on the opening day of EPCOT Center in Florida on October 1, 1982.

Traveling the World

Opposite:
The Expo City Marching Band (in foreground) faces the Trojan Marching Band with Song Girls between them in a "battle of the bands" during Expo '88 in Brisbane, Australia. This was the first year the band took a summer trip internationally. It happened at the urging of Barry Spanier, a Trojan Marching Band Alumnus, who was hired to form the Expo Marching Band. Bartner recalls, "The Australians played Waltzing Matilda *and then we played back* Stars and Stripes, *and it went back and forth, they would play their hottest tune and we'd play* Sing, Sing, Sing. *It was a marriage of two cultures—a great moment." The Trojans performed at a rugby match and toured Sydney before leaving Australia. The band played for three other Expos—in Seville, Spain in '92, Lisbon, Portugal in '98, and Aichi, Japan in '05.*

Left:
During the trip to Australia in 2000, the United States Ambassador to Australia was Genta Holmes, who also happened to be a USC Alumna. Dr. Bartner related, "We were giving a concert in front of the famous Sydney Opera House so we invited her to join my wife in a special guest box we had created. When the concert was over, she took the entire band on a dinner cruise of the harbor." He also told of how a USC Trustee in Hong Kong, Ronnie Chan, took the band on a harbor cruise on his private yacht to watch the New Year's fireworks display following their performance in the 2003 New Year's Parade. He added, "We were the only American band in the parade."

Right:
A performance at Sydney's Australian Rules Football match in the Sydney Cricket Grounds built in 1882.

The Trojan Marching Band under the direction of Dr. Arthur C. Bartner performing on Ipanema Beach in Rio de Janeiro, Brazil with the "Two Brothers" mountains visible in the background in 2008.

Overleaf, Pages 90-91:
In 2002, for the international summer trip, the Trojan Marching Band went to three capitals in Europe: Prague, Czech Republic; Vienna, Austria; and Budapest, Hungary. Here, they prepare to perform on the grounds of the residence of the United States Ambassador to the Czech Republic. They were invited to perform there at the invitation of First Lady Laura Bush who heard the band warming up in Prague's Old Town Square the day before.

Left:
The Trojan Marching Band performs near St. Stephen's Cathedral in the heart of Vienna, Austria. As the most important religious building in Austria's capital, the cathedral has born witness to many important events in that nation's history and has become one of the city's most recognizable symbols.

Right:
Because Dr. Bartner had to be in Nanjing, China for an international conference on entertainment, his wife took over the band's diplomatic duties. Here, Barbara Bartner (left) greets First Lady Laura Bush when the Trojans perform at the Ambassador's residence.

Marching toward Old Town Square, Prague, Czech Republic in 2002.

Performing in front of St. Stephens Cathedral in Vienna, Austria in 2002.

Left:
Dr. Bartner recalled that while the band was in France, they stopped and played in front of a church where a paratrooper had landed on the steeple and was stuck for a time. "It was a small town, Sainte Mére Èglise in France," Bartner explained, "and when we played for them, there was such an outpouring of emotion. Older people who had lived through World War II, came out and embraced members of the band. We had played Stars and Stripes Forever, *and it was one of those great moving moments."*

Opposite:
In 1994, on the 50th anniversary of D-Day, the band visited Omaha Beach where the Allies landed to begin the liberation of Europe during World War II. The band makes foreign excursions every other year.

Right:
In the middle of the concert, one of the town's citizens who had been in the resistance during the war came up to Bartner to show him a picture of himself back in 1944.

Opposite:
During the 1994 international summer trip, the band performed in Paris in the shadow of the Eiffel Tower.

Above:
In 1996, one of the band's performances was in the gazebo in Hyde Park, London.

Above:
On the band's longest European trip, 19 days in 1990, they played in the Grand Place in Brussels, Belgium.

Back to their roots—The Trojan Marching Band plays Conquest! *at the original Coliseum in Rome in 2006. "It was poignant because we play so often at the Los Angeles Coliseum," says Dr. Bartner.*

Opposite:
The march continues toward the Plaza Navonna the historic site of the Four Rivers Statue by Bernini. The city closed down traffic for the band so they could perform their concert.

Left:
Marching across the River Tiber with the ruins of the Castel Sant'Angelo in the background.

Left:
The band lined up in the courtyard of the Uffizi Palace in Florence, and then marched through the city past a statue of David (and others) to present a concert in the plaza

Above:
During their visit to Florence, the Trojan Marching Band marches into the Boboli Gardens, after crossing the Arno River. The Duomo is visible in the background.

Right:
A performance in the Plaza Signoria in Florence in front of the Fountain of Neptune by Ammannati.

Left:
While touring mainland China in 2004, the band made a day trip from Beijing to the Great Wall. They performed a concert in the shadow of the wall in Badaling, then climbed the wall for a performance of Conquest!

While in China, the band performed in both Shanghai and Xi'an, the latter being the home of the vast army of terra cotta warriors, and the Chinese put on an unbelievably beautiful show of costumes and pageantry for the band. Dr. Bartner adds, "In Xi'an, they also presented us with a key to the city—the first time that has ever happened to an American marching band. In Shanghai, the Chinese closed all the shops on the famous Nanjing street where we marched."

Right:
Dr. and Mrs. Bartner with Chinese officials walking to the presentation where they received the key to the city of X'ian.

Japan 2005, Dr. Bartner explains: "These international trips have become a big part of the band experience, it's a whole new dimension for us to be able to travel and take our American culture abroad."

In 2005, the Trojan Marching Band became the first marching band to perform at Tokyo DisneySea Park in Japan.

"On one of our trips, we visited England in 1996," explained Dr. Bartner, "shown here in Bristol playing a concert in front of Clifton Cathedral."

Right:
The band toured three-capitals of Europe,
visiting Vienna, Prague and Budapest.
Here, they play in front of a church
in Budapest.

Above:
"While in England," Dr. Bartner said, "the weather
was so bad, they allowed us to play our concert inside
Edinburgh Castle."

Dr. Bartner leads the Trojan Marching Band in a concert at the American Pavilion of the World Expo in Seville, Spain in 1992, one of the four World Expo's where the band performed.

A concert at an outdoor pavilion at the World Expo in Spain in 1992.

Below:
(left to right) Tony Fox, associate director and arranger of the Trojan Marching Band, Jack Wall, who created the July 4th event for Catalina, his wife Nita Wall, Barbara Bartner and Dr. Arthur C. Bartner have lunch at the Wrigley Mansion overlooking the Casino.

Above and Opposite:
The Trojan Marching Band makes its annual trip to Catalina Island to celebrate Independence Day, a tradition since 1990. The band marches down Crescent Avenue in a noon parade, then performs a concert at Wrigley Plaza in the afternoon and another that evening in the iconic casino ballroom.

In 1990, Dr. Bartner described, "We were the first college band to play in East Berlin when the Berlin Wall (shown above with band members) was torn down. The students were allowed to chisel off pieces of the wall to keep as souvenirs, along with their communist hats."

Members of the Trojan Marching Band snooze while waiting for baggage check-in at the SeaTac Airport on October 23, 2005.

Sports or Music?
...or Both

It was a beautiful morning on the campus of the University of Southern California on August 30, 1940. There was no indication that something had happened thousands of miles away that would have a profound effect on the athletic and music departments of the school. The event was the birth of Arthur C. Bartner in Maplewood, New Jersey.

A youthful Arthur C. Bartner (right) with his sister and younger brother.

Bartner playing trumpet at age 16.

Bartner at age 10.

Bartner (number four) on his high school basketball team.

Bartner, the high school basketball star, takes a shot.

A high school class photo.

No one in Maplewood, New Jersey had any inkling that the birth of a boy in 1940 would have an impact on the music world or the University of Southern California, least of all the proud parents, Mark and Bess Bartner. Little Art Bartner was in the fourth grade before something stirred in him to pick up his older brother's trumpet and ask to take lessons.

Just two years later, he garnered his first taste of audience approval when he played *Oh Holy Night* at a Christmas concert to enthusiastic applause. Music was coming naturally to him and he liked it. By the time he was in junior high school, he was also playing the piano. His band director convinced him to take up the euphonium (a member of the tuba family), but lugging that instrument in parades was not to his taste so he left that in its case one Memorial Day and marched playing his trumpet, which he had been keeping up with private lessons.

It was about that same time that he first heard the U.S. Marine Corps Band. "I was in the ninth grade, and I can remember to this day they played *Bugler's Holiday*," Bartner says, "and a light went on in my head—my thought was that if I could play like that, I could do that for the rest of my life."

When he was chosen to play in the New Jersey All-State Orchestra, one of their first concerts was Tchaikovsky's *Fourth Symphony*. The realization that sitting inside an ensemble, being able to make that kind of music and create that kind of excitement pretty much closed the deal for him that music would be his career.

But on the other hand, he was a serious athlete along with his musical talents. In his junior year in high school, he made the New Jersey All-State basketball team. So he had a dilemma—a career in sports or music? As it has turned out, athletic ability and interest has been a major plus along with his music as a band director.

By the time he was ready for college, he had many choices available: Curtis School of Music, Julliard, University of Rochester-Eastman, or the University of Michigan. The latter was his choice because as he says, "I wanted a well-rounded college life. I still hadn't decided I wanted to be a band director. I was dreaming that I could maybe be a professional basketball player, or a jazz

Above:
Bartner with his trumpet in the University of Michigan Marching Band (from a newspaper clipping).

Below:
One of his first directing assignments was as leader of his fraternity glee club at the University of Michigan.

Below:
Bartner, playing trumpet and leading his dance-jazz band at the University of Michigan.

Right:
Bartner with some of his band members at North Adams High, his first teaching job.

musician, or play in an orchestra. It was a coincidence that Michigan had a great marching band."

When he went to the University of Michigan, he began to realize that there were great basketball players around him, and although he was talented, he didn't feel he could compete. He says, "I wasn't tall enough or fast enough." The four years with the UofM marching band was a great experience though, and led him to his career choice of band director.

He graduated from Michigan in 1962 and immediately married his sweetheart, Barbara Ann Masin whom he had first dated back in junior high. He continued his studies and received his Masters Degree in 1963. That same year, his son Steven was born.

He took his first job with a small high school of 225 students in North Adams, Michigan. He was the music teacher not only for the high and middle school, but also for fifth and sixth grades, and he was the band director—in short, he was responsible for everything musical at the school. What amazed him was the fact that the band had some 60 members. For such a small school, a surprising number. "The place reminded me of Meredith Willson's *The Music Man*; it was a very rural setting."

The sports program didn't have any kind of stadium or stands. He described it as being like a drive-in movie. The cars parked around the playing field on a bluff to watch the games and the band perform. If they liked the show, they would honk their horns. Once when there was a power failure, they turned on their car headlights to see the activities. "I spent two years there," he says, "a great place to learn how not to make mistakes." His daughter, Debbie, was born there.

The next five years were spent as the band director in Davison, Michigan, another relatively small community, but a suburb of the more populous Flint. The film maker Michael Moore played the clarinet in the band at that school, and graduated in 1972.

When Bartner started there, they had one band of about 60 members. By the time he left, they had three bands at the high school level and a marching band of 120, and the program was considered one of the best in the state. During that same time period, Bartner was completing his class work, prelims and tests for his doctorate—everything but the dissertation was done.

On January 1, 1970, the University of Southern California played football against the University of Michigan. USC won the game, but the UofM won the battle of the bands. USC was searching for a new band director, and USC's Dean of the Music School, Dr. Grant Beglarian, had gone to Michigan. Another classmate of Bartner's at UofM, Bob Wojciak was working on his doctorate at USC. "In fact," says Bartner, "we had marched together in the Michigan band." Not surprisingly, Wojciak

123

recommended Bartner to fill the post. Since most of the west coast potential candidates were not interested because the USC band had such a low reputation, the search widened enough to include the young man teaching in Michigan.

When Bartner arrived at USC, there were 80 students in the band, mostly music majors. At that time the School of Music did not grant scholarships to wind players or percussionists without being in the marching band. As a result, there were a lot of disgruntled students who didn't want to be in the marching band, but wanted the money. There was a second problem: for big games, the school would stack the band with junior college and high school kids, literally anyone to fill the ranks. So the band could go from 80 to 140 on game day with many more players who didn't want to be there—hardly a recipe for success.

It's not surprising that there was little interest in the band, no support from alumni, and the student body could not have cared less—and the reputation was extremely poor. What's more, they only performed at home games with the exception of going across town to UCLA and upstate for the Stanford or Cal games on alternate years.

That first fall season, along with the legendary assistant coach Marv Goux, Bartner revolutionized the "jock rally," a Friday afternoon before game days get together where the Trojan Marching Band rallied with the football team. As the season began, Bartner also introduced more current musical hits to the band's repertoire, such as Chicago's *Make Me Smile*.

When Notre Dame played USC that November, Bartner arranged for Hollywood composer Henry Mancini to guest conduct the Trojan Marching Band at the half-time show playing the *March of the Cue Balls* from the popular television series, *Mr. Lucky*. In spite of a steady downpour, the performance was filmed and used the following spring in a television special, *Monsanto Presents Mancini*. The band was taking on new importance.

In his second season, the improved performance stimulated more special appearances for the Trojan Marching Band, performing for the first time at Disneyland as part of the *I Am an American* ceremony celebrating the birthdays of Washington and Lincoln. They filmed their first television commercial for Beech Nut gum at the Coliseum, and Meredith Willson, composer of *The Music Man*, was a guest conductor for the amassed bands and the Trojans for High School Band Day. For the first time, female students were allowed to join the band. And new uniforms designed by the Walt Disney Company were introduced.

Another celebrity played with the band in 1972—Louie Bellson performed his *Carnaby Street* hit as part of the Salute to Big Band Drummers at half-time of the Notre Dame game.

On January 1, 1973, USC went to the Rose Bowl to play Ohio State. This was Dr. Bartner's first Rose Parade and Rose Bowl. An added bonus: Diana Ross performed with the band at half-time singing *Our Love Is Here to Stay* from

*Left:
The uniforms of the Trojan Marching Band in the early seventies.*

*Right:
Bartner leading his new members of the Trojan Marching Band at band camp in the early seventies.*

*Right:
In the late
seventies,
Bartner formed
a mass band to
open the baseball
season at Dodger
Stadium.*

*Below:
At Disneyland in
California, Bartner
leads a band of
students from
around the country.*

her movie, *Lady Sings the Blues*. USC beat Ohio State 42-17 claiming the National Championship. With that kind of national exposure, it's not surprising that 2000 fans turned out for a rally at the Arco Plaza in downtown Los Angeles before the USC – Oklahoma game at the Coliseum, the first USC football rally in downtown Los Angeles in 42 years.

By 1973, there were about 120 in the band when one of the students named Ken Dye came up with the idea that the band should travel with the football team to South Bend, Indiana for the Notre Dame game.

Bartner elaborated, "Up until that time, the band's trips were limited to the Stanford and University of California games and that was it. We had to raise the money for the trip, but we did it. Now we had been evolving a contemporary style for the band, and when we did our half-time show, one of the numbers we played was Edgar Winter's *Frankenstein*, a very popular tune of that period, with the song girls dancing on the field. This was in the heart of the mid-west, the epitome of collegiate football conservatism. The crowd was in total shock, but gave us a three minute standing ovation when they finished. That was the beginning of our road trips to South Bend, Indiana."

The trip to Notre Dame required traveling to Chicago, and while they were in that city, Mayor Daley invited the Trojan Marching Band to play a noon rally in the Civic Center. That has become a tradition as well.

That same season, Neil Diamond appeared with the band at the half-time of the USC-UCLA game with the Trojan Marching Band performing *Dear Father*, music Diamond had composed for the film, *Jonathan Livingston Seagull*.

For the second New Year's Day in a row, the Trojan Marching Band was at the Rose Bowl with USC battling Ohio State again, unfortunately losing the game this time. The band performed with the popular funk band, Tower of Power, playing their hit tune, *So Very Hard to Go*.

That summer, Bartner accepted the post as director of the All American College Band at Disneyland, which began a three-decade-long association with the park. College students from all over the country audition for the chance to play in the group for the summer season.

During that fall's football season, one the most exciting games was with the top-ranked Notre Dame. The Trojan Marching Band never stopped supporting the USC team even when they were behind by 24 points at the half. Tailback Anthony Davis spurred the comeback with a touchdown catch just before the half-time, and then a 3rd quarter opening kickoff return for another. USC ended up winning over the Irish 55-24.

During the half-time of that game, Robert Goulet joined the Trojan Marching Band to sing music from his film, *The Little Prince*. During the pre-game, his wife, Carol Lawrence, sang *The Star Spangled Banner* with the band.

More network television exposure came that year when Bartner and the band were invited to appear on the *Dinah!* Christmas special with Dinah Shore and Rock Hudson.

For the third year in a row, USC would play against Ohio State in the Rose Bowl on January 1, 1975 with the Trojans winning 18-17. The band's theme for the half-time show was *Make Your Own Kind of Music* and featured *Give It One* by Maynard Ferguson and *Dance to the Music* by Sly and Family Stone.

"Seventy-five seemed to be a banner year for us," explained Bartner, "we released our first Trojan Marching Band album that included many of our new sounds such as *Give It One* and Elton John's *The Bitch is Back*, as well as the distinctive arrangement of the *Stars and Stripes Rock* which is still popular today."

He continued, "Then the band provided 75 of Mitzi Gaynor's men (in tuxedos, not band uniforms) for her special, *Mitzi and 100 Guys.* Soon after that, MGM called on us for the opening of *That's Entertainment, Part II,* our first motion picture."

Later that year, the Trojan Marching Band performed in the Liberty Bowl with famed opera star Marguerite Piazza singing the National Anthem, and a half-time show with an elaborate patriotic theme celebrating America's Bicentennial. USC won over Texas A&M 20-0, bringing coach John McKay's 16 years at USC to a successful conclusion.

"In 1979, the Trojan Marching Band finally became the band as it is known today," Bartner went on, "with the recording of *Tusk*. We were coming off a National Championship season of 1978 under coach John Robinson, and during the summer of 1979, the band recorded *Tusk* in Dodger Stadium with Fleetwood Mac. The video was shown regularly on MTV and the album went platinum— the Trojan Marching Band had finally arrived."

Dr. Bartner continued, "One of the ultimate rewards of my job is when guys who come back and stop me and say, 'being in the marching band was the single greatest experience I had in four years at USC'. My second reward is when someone comes back and says 'I want to apologize for what I did in such and such a year because I really love this band, and now I understand what you were trying to do.' And I can't remember what he's apologizing for that happened some thirty or forty years ago, and I thank him for four great years."

Opposite:
The Trojan Marching Band on the field at Dodger Stadium for the recording of Tusk *with Fleetwood Mac, whose members are in the foreground, (left to right) Stevie Nicks, John McVie, Christine McVie, and Mick Fleetwood.*

Below:
The first platinum album for the Trojan Marching Band was Tusk *with Fleetwood Mac. Here, Dr. Bartner is seen conducting on the outfield of Dodger Stadium with headphones to listen to the tracks of the Fleetwood Mac recording. The music video was one of the first in regular rotation on the MTV network when it was launched in 1981.*

The Cerritos Concerts

In the mid-1980's, the Trojan Concert Band began performing spring "pops" concerts at places like Paramount Studios and Pickfair. As a result, one of the band's staunch supporters, Doug Padelford, invited Dr. Bartner to bring the band to Cerritos Center for the Performing Arts. The first concert in April of 1997 featured acclaimed composer and producer David Foster. Since then, the concerts have become an annual event, attracting such talents as Monica Mancini, Henry Winkler, Elmer Bernstein, Patti Austin, Michael Kamen, and many others.

Above:
The finale of the Pops in Cerritos Concert in 1997 featuring both the Concert Band and the Trojan Marching Band, the Silks and Twirlers.

Opposite:
The same concert, Dr. Bartner salutes the Song Girls, band alumni and the performers.

Michael Kamen guest conducts the Trojan Marching Band and the Concert Band at the 1998 Cerritos Concert.

Left:
David Foster, who composed the film music for Bodyguard, *gets his Trojan helmet from Dr. Bartner honoring his work as guest artist at the 1997 Cerritos concert.*

Below:

At Cerritos in 2000, an impressive group of film composers joined Dr. Bartner (far right) and his band manager Dan Schwartz (far left) who produced the show that year. They were (right to left): David Raksin, Bruce Broughton, Alfred Newman's widow, Martha, Tommy Newman, Buddy Baker, Basil Poledouris.

Left:
Oscar winner Elmer Bernstein conducted the Concert Band in Cerritos in 1999. Bernstein won his Academy Award for Thoroughly Modern Millie.

Right:
Marilyn McCoo, who is not only a solo artist, but also is a member of the Fifth Dimension and works with her husband Billy Davis, Jr., performed at the 2000 Cerritos concert. She has won eight Grammys.

Conquest! A Salute to Alfred Newman and His Film Legacy *was the title of the Cerritos Concert for 2000. Here we see Traveler joining the audience for the finale with the band in the boxes above.*

Above and opposite:
Two views of the concert band joined with the marching band at the Cerritos 2001 concert titled The Spirit of America.

Left:
Dr. Arthur C. Bartner greets Paul Salamunovich, director of the St. Charles Borromeo Choir, which joined the Concert band for America the Beautiful (below) *at the 2002 Cerritos Concert.*

Above: Dr. Bartner conducts soprano Anya Matanovic and the band at Cerritos 2002.

The Spirit of Troy on Broadway *was the theme of the 2003 Cerritos Pops Concert. (Clockwise from top left) Dr. Arthur C. Bartner conducts the concert orchestra with Sharon Gless vocalizing; Dale Kristien; Michel Bell; Patti Austin receives a Trojan helmet from Dr. Bartner; John Charles; and Patti Austin.*

Remembering Mancini, *the Cerritos Concert of 2004 included guest stars (clockwise from above right) flutist Jim Walker, Plas Johnson on saxophone, vocalist Monica Mancini, and on harmonica, Tommy Morgan.*

Henry Winkler received an honorary helmet (above) at the 2006 Cerritos concert.

The 2005 Pops at Cerritos concert featured guest artists Louis Bellson (above) on drums and trombonist Bill Watrous (right). The theme for 2005 was All That Jazz.

Right:
A typical finale for a Cerritos concert involves the band marching through the auditorium to the stage.

The tenth pops concert in 2006 at Cerritos titled Celebration *under the baton of Dr. Arthur C. Bartner (near right) and guest star Monica Mancini. Barbara Morrison was another guest star with the concert band (left). (far right) Both the Trojan Marching Band and the Concert band filled the hall with music with the Song Girls in front.*

Art
for
Art's Sake

Art for Art's Sake

by

Robert W. Jensen

I can remember clearly the first time I experienced the Trojan Marching Band under the direction of Dr. Arthur C. Bartner. It was at a charity gala in Beverly Hills. The band made its entrance and the ballroom came to life. I made a mental note that I should try to paint them and capture that wonderful joy that surrounds them.

After voicing that desire to my friend and columnist Bonnie Churchill, and being the woman of action that she is, I had a call from her about a week later telling me "to grab my sketch book," that we were heading downtown where Dr. Bartner had the band assembled for an opening and he had agreed to come early for a "sitting." The painting titled Concert in the Shade was the result.

About a year later, I was going through my phone messages after returning from a trip to Paris where Galerie Marumo was exhibiting my work at the time. There was a request to call a person in the Trojan Marching Band office at USC. I learned that they were going to honor Dr. Bartner's 20th anniversary with the band, and they wanted a portrait of him in action. When I requested another "sitting," they asked what I was doing on New Years.

Two weeks later, I found myself with the band on field at the Rose Bowl. And since the portrait and honors were a secret from Dr. Bartner, I was there as a reporter doing a story on the band, so I could make my sketches and take some photographs without alerting him. The portrait was a huge success with him, the band and his fans.

Since then, every once in a while, I would get a call asking me if I'd like to be involved in another Trojan project. My answer has always been "yes," since being around this group is like bathing in the fountain of youth. A number of paintings have been done over the years, and at the 25th anniversary, I helped produce a book with many of the works included. At one point, I produced a statue of Tommy Trojan which was presented to many of the band's major supporters.

Top Left:
Robert W. Jensen's first painting of the band, as they appeared at an opening of the Convention Center in downtown Los Angeles.
1986 Acrylic on canvas, 62"X 62".

Left:
The first portrait of Dr. Arthur C. Bartner by Jensen which was done for his 20th anniversary celebration with the Trojan Marching Band.
1990 Acrylic on canvas, 40"X 30".

Right:
USC Homecoming
by Jensen.
watercolor on
paper, 48"X 52".

Left:
Pep Rally *is a painting by Robert W. Jensen, acrylic on canvas.*

Right:
Trojan Victory *following a win at the Rose Bowl in Pasadena.*

Left:
Cardinal and Gold, Red, White and Blue—*a painting by Jensen of the Fourth of July celebration at Catalina Island in 2004.*

Right:
The artist, Robert W. Jensen with some sketches of Dr. Bartner.

Above:
Catalina Fourth, *another painting of the Trojans at Catalina.*

Left:
Trojans at Muckenthaler, *a painting of Jensen's exhibition and USC rally at the museum in Orange County in 2006.*

Scrap Book

A Letter from Paul McDonald
USC Quarterback 1976-1979
Currently color commentator for
USC Football radio broadcast

My fondest memories as a football player at USC revolve around the Trojan Marching Band. They were very much a part of our game preparation. At practices the players all heard the band playing from Cromwell Field during game week.

Every Friday was especially cool as the band with the song girls would play for us on our practice field to get us relaxed for the game the next day. The players and even some of the coaches would get into the act as they would strut their stuff to the music the band played.

And then, on game day I would get chills down my spine when I heard *Conquest!* as we walked down the tunnel to take on our opponent. To this day, I still get emotional when I listen to the band since it takes me back in time...to maybe the best time of my life at USC!

Yes, "The Spirit of Troy" was interwoven into the fabric of my team in the late 70's, and today, they are synonymous with what it is to be a Trojan. Thank you, Dr. Bartner for your commitment to the Trojans over the last 40 years and for creating so many wonderful memories I will never forget.

Paul McDonald—All American 1979

Left:
Dr. Karl D. Swearingen, an associate director of the Trojan Marching Band for eight years, was also an assistant professor of music at the Thornton School of Music. Here, he was introduced at one of the Cerritos Concerts.

Opposite:
Players, song girls, members of the band—all dance to All Right Now *at one of the traditional Friday jock rallies.*

156

Right:
USC football coach, John Robinson (1976-1982) and (1993-97) leads the team with the band in the Coliseum rallying after a game.

Left:
In 1994, famed trumpeter Arturo Sandoval performed Mambo Caliente with the band at the halftime of a Notre Dame game.

Right:
Singer Thom Yorke (center) and guitarist Jonny Greenwood (in white shirt) of Radiohead with the Trojan Marching Band after the Grammys in 2009.

Above:
Maynard Ferguson plays trumpet with the Trojan Marching Band in 1977.

Right:

Dr. Bartner explains, "Band camp began in 1970 with my arrival. The whole purpose is to teach freshmen how to be Trojans, to work hard, to support each other, and the team. We cheer from the first play to the last play, no matter what the score, or how many people leave early, we cheer and of course, we play the fight songs. At band camp they learn the fundamentals of marching and the spirit of what it takes to be a Trojan. This happens each August, ten days before the beginning of USC's fall semester. More than 65 hours of practice are invested by members during this time and hundreds more are spent by the band staff — recruiting, planning, and organizing the camp for the more than 125 freshmen and 175 returning members. The band practices daily during that week and a half — days that last from 8:00 a.m. to 10:00 p.m. A typical day has the band marching for six hours on the field and practicing three more in music rehearsal."

Left:
A U.S. Navy SEAL descends on the USC Trojan Marching Band in a pregame performance at the Coliseum.

Above:
Dr. Arthur C. Bartner with the President of the
University of Southern California, Dr. Steven B. Sample.

A Letter from Dr. Steven B. Sample

Dr. Art Bartner is more than the best band director in the nation; he's a Trojan legend, an icon, an institution. Over the last 40 years he's put the spirit in The Spirit of Troy, and he's made the Trojan Marching Band a symbol of pride and excellence for the entire university.

Right:
For a half-time show at the Coliseum in 1996, Larry Harmon,
who was a drum major for the USC band in 1950, and went on
to originate Bozo the Clown, joined Dr. Bartner and the current
drum major after Bozo leaped out of bass drum while the band
played the Bozo theme song.

160

Above:
(left to right) Ted Tollner, football coach, his wife, Barbara,
Stan Morrison, basketball coach, with Dr. Bartner at
a "Pops at Pickfair" event.

Left:
Dr. Jerry Buss, owner of the Lakers, receives an award from Dr. Bartner at one of the "Pops at Pickfair" concerts that the Trojan Marching Band performed at the famous residence built by early film stars, Mary Pickford and Douglas Fairbanks. Buss owned the property for several years.

Below:
Members of the Trojan Marching Band make up an ensemble for Dr. Buss, called the Laker Band, shown at the Staples Center.

A Letter from Dr. Jerry Buss

I've always gotten great enjoyment from the intensity of the atmosphere at college football and basketball games. An energy that I thought was missing at Laker and all NBA games. The band, the cheerleaders, rooting for your team was an environment that I wanted to create at our games, for our fans, and for our players. One of the first things I did as owner of the Lakers was to create the Laker Girls and get the USC Band involved.

The band and the Laker Girls accomplished my goals of energizing the crowd and our players and are a big part of the creation of our unique sports brand of "Showtime."

I thank Art Bartner for the spirit he brings to his work on behalf of his bandsmen, the University, and for his part in making the band a part of the Laker dynamic.

Right:
Wearing a jersey with the number forty, Dr. Bartner celebrated his fortieth year as director of the USC Trojan Marching Band at Dodger Stadium at the USC Night Game on September 14, 2009. The band played The Star Spangled Banner *before the game and* God Bless America *during the 7th inning stretch.*

Left:
Dr. Bartner shares a moment with famed producer David Wolper and legendary baseball coach Rod Dedeaux (right). In his 45-year tenure at USC (1942-86), Dedeaux led the Trojans to 11 College World Series crowns and 28 conference titles. He posted an overall collegiate record of 1,332-571-11 for a .699 winning percentage. He retired with more wins than any other college baseball coach (he currently ranks seventh among Division I coaches). After retiring, he served as USC's director of baseball.

A letter from Ronnie Lott

Dr. Bartner had the same intensity and drive for perfection in leading the Spirit of Troy marching band that Howard Jones, John McKay and John Robinson did in leading the USC football team to nine National Championships. Those coaches instilled greatness in their players year after year and Dr. Bartner has done the same with his band members. He embodies all the same attributes those great USC coaches had.

Above:
Dr. Bartner with defensive back Ronnie Lott, who, during his years at USC (1977-1980), helped the team to a share of the 1978 national championship and played in the 1979 and 1980 Rose Bowls. Lott was a unanimous All-American and team captain in 1980. He was inducted in 2002 as one of 15 new members of the College Football Hall of Fame, and was also a 1995 inductee to the USC Athletic Hall of Fame.

Above:
Julie Kohl (seated), whose off–campus Trojan Barrel restaurant was a USC institution, helped Dr. Bartner and staff break ground for the new Juliette Kohl Trojan Band Center in 1994.

Left:
Doug Pardee, a USC Trustee and staunch supporter of the Trojan Marching Band with Dr. Bartner.

Left:
As Hollywood's band, it was only natural for USC Alum, Robert Zemeckis who was directing the movie Forrest Gump *in 1994, to ask the Trojan Marching Band to portray the 60's Alabama Band in the film. In one scene where Forrest Gump runs toward them, they flash him some decidedly Trojan victory signs. The film is one of twelve in which the Trojan Marching Band has appeared during Dr. Bartner's tenure.*

Right:
Sid Caesar posed with band members on the set of Grease II.

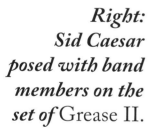

Above:
In 2007, Alex Trebek, host of the Jeopardy *television show put on the helmet and posed as Tommy Trojan during the college championship series.*

Left:
(left to right)
Corky and John
McKay, John and
Linda Robinson
and Art and
Barbara Bartner.

A letter from John Robinson

Art and the band saved my job!! I had lost my first game and things were very tense. We were uptight practicing for the next game.

Halfway through that Friday practice the band came marching through the gate and started to play!! Suddenly a female band member grabbed one of the players and started to dance! Pretty soon everyone was dancing!

I thought, "This is bad! My team gets embarrassed and now I have dancing with the team!"

However, it broke the negative mood and we went on to win eleven games and the Rose Bowl.

Thanks, Art! And especially thanks to that band member!

Below:
Dr. Bartner with Ken Cotler, a USC Alumnus who raised money for the band with events at his house called "Up the Irish." He traveled all over the world on the band trips. Here, he is with Dr. Bartner in Edinburgh, Scotland.

Right:
Heisman Trophy winner Marcus Allen, one of USC's great running backs with Dr. Bartner.

Billed as the largest outdoor live entertainment show held in the United States, Dr. Bartner leads a 1,000-piece mass band at the Tenth Pan American Games Opening Ceremony at the Indianapolis Motor Speedway in 1987.

Right:
Anthony Davis (28) was a college football All-American in 1974, and led the USC Trojans in rushing, scoring and kick return yardage for three consecutive seasons. He is long remembered for scoring 11 touchdowns in three games against Notre Dame. In a 45-23 USC win on December 2, 1972, he scored six touchdowns which set a school single game record.

Above:
Dr. Bartner with Lisa Leslie at the Coliseum. Lisa made All-American her last three years with the Women of Troy, and was USA Basketball's Player of the Year in 1993 as a junior.

A letter from Anthony Davis

The thing that I remember more than anything about Dr. Bartner is his energy. At the 1974 Notre Dame game, the greatest game in school history, I ran in tune with him and the Trojan Marching Band. The way he ran the band was like a field general. He was a coach just like John McKay. I will always remember his high energy and how he, like me, continuously strives for perfection.

167

Left:
The Trojan Marching Band's 10-piece ensemble, consisting of four trumpets, three trombones, bass drum, snare drum and tuba player, played at the wedding of Craig and Susan Caldwell, both USC Alumni and supporters of the band. The 10-piece band receives more than 600 requests for appearances in a year, and completes at least half of them while traveling some 14,000 miles. In addition to weddings, the requests are for birthdays, bar mitzvahs, anniversaries, corporate conferences, media events, and of course, university events. The 10-piece is performing somewhere, including on boats (below), almost every day.

Right:
At the 2004 Cerritos Concert, Remembering Mancini, a long time supporter of the Trojan Marching Band was greeted by the Bartners. (left to right) Herb Nootbaar, Barbara Bartner, Elinor Nootbaar, and Dr. Bartner.

At Homecoming, November 4, 1995, for the final celebration of the Year of the Band, over 750 band alums joined the 250 current band members to form the largest Trojan Marching Band ever assembled. Together they formed a massive USC on the field and blasted out the fight songs.

A mass band led by Dr. Bartner performed at the Democratic National Convention in 1992 held in Madison Square Garden in New York City.

Left:
Rodney Peete leads the Trojan Marching Band in Conquest! *after the USC-UCLA game where he led the Trojans back from a 12-0 3rd quarter deficit to a 17-13 win, which cinched the Trojans a berth in the Rose Bowl in 1987.*

Rodney Peete with Dr. Bartner at Swim with Mike.

A Letter from Mike Garrett

Marv Goux taught me, as a student-athlete, the importance of the Trojan Marching Band and Dr. Arthur C. Bartner. Their legacy is forever intertwined with the great heritage of the University of Southern California. On behalf of all the student-athletes, coaches and the National Championships, Art, We Thank You.

Above:
Dr. Bartner with Mike Garrett, current USC Athletic Director, who was a USC tailback from 1963-65, and a Heisman Trophy winner in 1965.

A Letter from Rodney Peete

Many things inspired me to attend USC. The academics, the tradition, the athletic program and of course the band. I remember being a ball boy for the Arizona Wildcats in 1980 and USC came to Tucson for the first time. I was in awe of the players but I was inspired by the USC Band.

I was hooked at 14 years old. Fast forward to 1987 and USC vs UCLA. We were big underdogs and the winner of that game, won the Pac 10 and was on their way to the Rose Bowl. We came back in the fourth quarter and won the game in dramatic fashion.

As time ran out and we all were saluting our fans, Art Bartner asked me to climb the ladder and direct the band in Conquest. I still get chills and that will go down as one of my favorite memories of all time. Congratulations Art and thank you for all your inspiration.

Any USC Game, Anywhere

If a USC Athletic team needs the Trojan Marching Band anywhere, at any time, The Spirit of Troy will answer the call. Beyond the gridiron, the band regularly performs at more than 75 games, matches, and meets each year.

Swimming, water polo, baseball, crew, volleyball, track, tennis, and basketball are just some of the sports at which the band performs.

The Trojan Marching Band also regularly travels with its teams when they reach the postseason. The Spirit of Troy traveled to the 2007 NCAA Women's Soccer College Cup in College Station, Texas to cheer the team on to its first national title in soccer.

It has also been to the Men's Water Polo National Championship Games — 1998, 2006, 2007, and 2008 — the 2004 and 2008 Women's Water Polo National Championship matches, the Men's Volleyball Championship in 2009 and the Women's Volleyball Championships in 2000, 2002, 2003, 2004, and 2007.

And whenever the men's or women's basketball teams makes the "Big Dance," the band is there, including appearances at the men's 2001 East Regional in Philadelphia and the 2006 East Regional in East Rutherford, New Jersey. The band has also traveled to the NIT and WNIT.

A Letter from John Naber
USC Class of 1977 - 1976 Olympic Swimmer - Winner of 4 Gold Medals, 1 Silver Medal

My freshman year, when USC was a powerhouse of the gridiron, swimming often took a back seat to the "revenue sports" but every time we hosted a swim meet on our campus, the "Spirit of Troy" Trojan Marching Band always sent a contingent to play for the swimmers. The indoor natatorium dubbed "the dungeon" with water-spitting gargoyles in the corners of the pool, was infamous for its acoustics. A bass drum, two snare drums, a trumpet and a trombone would make enough noise to sound like a full orchestra. The intimidation factor of having the band was equal to winning three individual races, and the USC swimmers always swam faster when they felt the chills of hearing *Conquest!* before their races. When USC won the national title that year over Indiana University, our margin of victory was one point… and I think the USC Marching Band deserves a lot of credit for that.

At some schools, being a member of the marching band is somewhat less than a stellar honor. Marching around in thick, hot uniforms, carrying heavy instruments, and anonymous until you screw up, it's usually a thankless job. But in my undergraduate years, when most of the kids in the dorms were playing rock and roll tunes, the word got out that the Trojan Marching Band was joining with Fleetwood Mac to record one of its greatest hits. It was the title tune of their album, "Tusk." (I always tend to spell the name of the song, "tUSC.") When we purchased the popular album, and heard the distinctive sounds of the Spirit of Troy, our hearts swelled with pride: "Hey, that's us!" Dr. Bartner made it cool to be a part of the Trojan Marching Band (and it still is).

All my home football games took place in the LA Coliseum, and the USC Marching Band was always a big part of that experience. Though I was (and still am) proud of our band, I always felt that in the Coliseum, they were playing not for me, but for the players on the football field. In 1984, I was honored with the privilege of carrying the Olympic flag into the LA Coliseum for the Opening Ceremony of the 1984 Olympic Games, and prior to marching around the track, I noticed Dr. Bartner leading not one, but the equivalent of eight marching bands in unison playing some of the country's most patriotic songs, and marching some of the most sophisticated routines I had ever seen on the field. On that day, I knew that they were playing for me (and the other Olympians, of course).

When my daughter was a junior in high school, I took her to an Olympic event in San Diego at the Sea World theme park. Fortunately, the USC Marching Band was scheduled to perform that day, and I noticed the friendly smile of Dr. Bartner as he led the group off the busses heading toward the dressing rooms. I introduced him to my daughter, and when he found out she was in the process of choosing her next school, he gave an almost invisible signal to the band members, and as

a group, they formed a circle around my daughter and began to play Conquest! What seemed like ten to twelve drummers, a dozen horns and a ton of enthusiasm penetrated my daughter's ears with the most authentic kind of "surround-sound." USC promptly moved to the top of her list of potential schools.

Each April since 1984, the University of Southern California has hosted the annual "Swim With Mike" fundraiser at the McDonalds Olympic Swim Stadium, site of the 1984 Olympic swimming events. "Swim with Mike" and the "Disabled Student Athlete Scholarship Fund" assist high school athletes who, through illness or injury, are no longer able to compete athletically. This 30-year campaign named after a USC swimming teammate, Mike Nyeholt, has raised over ten million dollars for scholarships and expenses to allow dozens of students to pursue their higher education goals and dreams. Each year's highlight is the presentation of awards to the charity's outstanding volunteers, donors and exceptional scholarship recipients. Balloon arches cover the pool as people swim laps to raise funds, football players race cheerleaders in inner-tube relays, students exhibit their clown diving and belly-flop skills, and the event always ends with a full outdoor barbeque feast.

Interestingly, the program cannot begin until Dr. Bartner and the "Spirit of Troy" Trojan Marching Band arrives en masse, to kick-off the festivities. I have served as the Master of Ceremonies over twenty times, and without fail, it is the mustachioed face of Dr. Bartner that lets me know this program and that day's events are truly special. Once the band is situated in the grandstands, I catch a smile from Dr. Bartner, because he knows I am going to introduce my favorite band of all. "Ladies and Gentlemen," I say, "Once again, led by USC's famous Dr. Arthur C. Bartner, it's The Spirit of Troy, Trojan Marching Band," and on cue, the glorious sound fills the arena.

For my four undergraduate years, I was reminded to always address my swim coach, Peter Daland, as "Coach" or "Coach Daland" or Mr. Daland. We never referred to him as "Peter." Now that I have my diploma, I am happy to put my arm around his shoulders and say, "How's it going, Peter?" With Dr. Bartner, I always felt that I could give him a handshake or a hug, but I would never say, "Hi there, Art." For me, he will always be, "Dr. Bartner."

There is not a time at a football game, charity event, pep rally or fundraiser where I catch Dr. Bartner's eye that he does not take the time to smile and wave back and acknowledge our common past. With some people, you share the school for four years. For forty years, Dr. Bartner has personified the phrase, "He's a Trojan for Life!" God Bless Dr. Arthur C. Bartner!!

Above:

(left to right) Lynn Swann, Dr. Bartner, and Marv Goux. Dr. Bartner credits Marv Goux with, "teaching me what it means to be a Trojan," says Bartner, "starting with the importance of the Notre Dame game, but let me give you an example. It was 1970, my first year at USC, and Marv was really one of the few guys that paid attention to me and to the band. He established what's known as the jock rally—before every home game, the team and band get together for school songs and Marv getting up and giving an unbelievably great pep talk. At one of these rallies, he got up and started to dance in the middle of one our songs, and then the team started to dance, and the song girls, and everybody was dancing—the start of another tradition. And Marv started the idea of a senior team member conducting the band, Lynn Swann, who made All-American in 1973, was the first to conduct The Lone Ranger." *Bartner added, "Marv was a great assistant coach under Mc Kay and Robinson. He taught everyone what 'Fight On' means—basically that you never give up."*

A Letter from Lynn Swann
Class of 1974 - National Champions - Football - 1972
All-American 1973

What a great 40-year run, and growing, it has been. As a freshman in 1970 and graduate in 1974, you and the band were the exclamation mark on two Rose Bowls and a National Championship in 1972! Those years were just part of the history that gives us just cause to have and play the music *Conquest!*

I have such vivid memories of the band playing in our dungeon locker rooms in the Physical Education Building. All the band members, players and coaches shoulder to shoulder, sweating, playing the music and cheering to defeat the weekend opponent. There was nothing like it anywhere but at USC. The late Marv Goux could always blend the music and inspirational words as only a Trojan and ex-Marine could do. Fight on!

Certainly Art, it was a unique pleasure to be the first player to lead the band after the last practice prior to the game. I think the horn players' cheeks are still sore from what had to be the slowest version of *Conquest!* ever directed. We picked up the tempo on the next game and now a player leads the band with sword in hand. Over 40 years, you have just made it better each year.

We all thank you for not just marking time, but creating lasting memories with musical performances on and off the field. You have spread the spirit of Troy across the nation and provided hope in hostile stadiums. The University of Southern California, its administration, its teams, its students and its alumni owe you the utmost respect and gratitude for 40 years of brilliance. Hi Ho Traveler - Away!!

Excerpts from a 1995 Speech by Assistant Coach Marv Goux at the Silver Celebration for Dr. Arthur C. Bartner

The story I want to tell ya happened on October 20, 1979 and it happened in South Bend, Indiana when the University of Southern California played the University of Notre Dame in the great game of football. There were 59,075 people as there are at every game there because that's all it holds. That stadium was rockin' as it always rocks when the Trojans visit South Bend.

To those of you who have been there and have seen these games, you know what I'm talking about. And to those of you who haven't, you haven't lived yet. Now, this was one of those days where it's gonna be a "knock-down, drag-out" because they're a damn good football team but so are we. We got a Heisman Trophy winner in Charlie White, we got Brad Budde, Myron Lapka. We got a bunch of tough guys, and they got a bunch of tough guys.

We got a great band because the 'SC Band is now in the stands. They've been coming for a couple years but they're there and they're playing and they're playing through the whole game. And we're hammering Notre Dame and they're hammering us. It was back and forth and back and forth.

And it's about 21 to 19 or something like that. And all of the sudden, the fourth quarter comes and the Trojans come alive like we used to do and we can still do. We start pounding on these boys, we start hammering 'em, we start running the football and we start running it down their throat. And it's in the fourth quarter. We kept punching 'em and punching 'em and they drop those arms and then we let 'em have it.

Believe me, I never forget Charlie White coming up the sideline and he made about a 15-yard run. And over comes Bob Crable from Notre Dame and Waymer and he had a great shot on him, really hit him. Boom! Charlie jumps up, Brad Budde's there to pick him back up, and I watched those two guys down on the ground that just hit him and I said, "Hell, it's over, we got this one." We beat them 42 to 23 that day.

But the great thing, this day in my life I'll remember to the day I die was in the Notre Dame tunnel. I've been there 15 times: two as a player and 13 as a coach. And going out the tunnel, the Notre Dame band comes in there and they play the *Notre Dame Victory March*. But the 'SC band was right behind them. They got in there and they played *Fight On!* and *Conquest!* like it's never been played before. It was so damn good, it brought the players out of the locker room down there to see it and look at it. And our guys are screaming and yelling and the band is. And the

In 1973, the Trojan Marching Band made its first road trip to Notre Dame, and wowed the mid-western audience.

Notre Dame players come out of their locker room and they can't believe what's happening. We now own them. We own South Bend. They belong to us. And I could see in their players' eyes and so forth.

And they played so good and, Art, you and those guys were fabulous. And then the best part was, they walked out of the tunnel and they're yelling and screaming because they're crazy. And they took a right and I ran upstairs and I told the players, "Follow me." And, at Notre Dame, you open the door and, hell, you're outside. And we went out there and we watched 'em.

And as they took a right and they started to go - this was October - there were some clouds in the sky and the sun was setting. The clouds were cardinal and gold. Believe me! The trees were cardinal and gold. The band members had their hats off and they were holding them in the air. And they had their instruments and had towels and they were waving them around. And all you could hear was the roar of the drum. Boom... boom, boom... boom.

The Trojans had come and they had conquered. Now, to me, I think about that all the time and I thank you Art Bartner and I thank all the band members who've ever played *Fight On!* and *Conquest!* But I will always remember that day of October 20th 1979. Art Bartner, I love you.

Left:
1986 – Dr. Bartner shook hands with Mayor of Los Angeles, Tom Bradley following a concert on the City Hall steps.

Below:

Ralph and Trish Goodson received a helmet from Dr. Bartner in recognition of their support of the Trojan Marching Band. Says Bartner, "The Goodsons are typical of the great people I meet because of the band. They originally came to me because they wanted the band to play in their boat parade in Marina del Rey."

Left: Doug Padelford with his wife, Anita, are greeted by Dr. Bartner at the Cerritos Center for the Performing Arts.

Film stars James Stewart and Robert Wagner posed in Griffith Park with Trojan Band Members, Silks, and Song Girls during a charity marathon in the '90's.

Above:
Speaking about the Trojan Marching Band at the Three Tenors Concert *in Dodger Stadium, Los Angeles in 1994.* Dr. Bartner said, "To this day, I remember who was in the front row when the band marched in—Frank Sinatra, Gene Kelly, the who's who of the entertainment business—but then the concert itself with Plácido Domingo, Luciano Pavarotti, and José Carerras—Zubin Mehta conducting and Lalo Schifrin guest conducting. We played our tunes at intermission, but the band got to stay for the concert—it was amazing for all of us to be a part of this cultural event of the year."

A letter from James F. Ward

My initial introduction to Dr. Bartner was as a student athlete. I truly benefitted so much from my exposure to the USC music that years later I realized I had to give something back to the University Band and Dr. Bartner for the special pleasure given to me.

At my deepest level, there is an unwavering conviction that our USC music is the language that connects the past, the present, and leads us into the future within the USC family. Our USC music evokes an emotional response that means something different to everyone, yet something the same in our connection as "family." Regardless the level of our response, it is crystal clear that the response is real and measurable.

When Dr. Bartner and I formally met for the first time, I became a volunteer "Red Coat" at our home football games and selected bowl games, giving children and USC fans small gifts in the name of the band. Each Red Coat working game day has assigned duties and responsibilities. All of us are there to help Dr. Bartner, guiding the tens of thousands of fans who hear the Spirit of Troy on an enjoyable march to the Coliseum, continuing their enjoyment of the music during the games, delighting in the half-time performances and the post-game experience.

Our eldest son, a USC computer engineering graduate and former yell leader, married a USC psychology graduate with the wedding being held in Colonial Williamsburg, Virginia. I was given the pleasurable opportunity to act as one of the USC Trojan 10-Piece band, playing the trumpet and marching, parade like, through the town of Colonial Williamsburg to the location of the wedding reception. Since both the bride and groom hailed from distant locations in the United States, the guest list was primarily close family and their friends, almost all fellow USC graduates. The 10-Piece parade was being filmed and when the wedding guests realized what was happening and heard the music, the place went crazy! It has been thirteen years since that 10-Piece performance, and every time I watch the wedding video and the pure joy it brought to the wedding party and their guests, (not to mention the tourists who enjoyed the parade), it brings tears to my eyes. Fight On!

How does one thank Dr. Bartner, or even begin to explain what he has meant and the impact of what he has done? Perhaps the following paragraph sums up what he has created:

"A sudden hush covers the crowd as a lone Trojan warrior marches undaunted to the center of the historic Los Angeles Memorial Coliseum. His brass helmet shines as if on fire and his battle worn sword wields a spark of blinding light as he impales the ground below. The crowd begins to roar as if on cue and behind him, the Trojan Marching Band attentively awaits his command. The shrill of his whistle pierces the sound of 90,000 screaming fans and the thunderous cry of U-S-C consumes every part of the arena. As the band takes the field, filling every part of the gridiron, thousands of hands form the victory sign and mark time to *Tribute to Troy*. This is the epitome of excitement; this is the Spirit of Troy."

Above:
James F. Ward (center) exposed as a bogus member of the Trojan 10-piece band at his son's wedding.

Above:
Whoopi Goldberg began her good wishes for many more years of great music with "Congratulations, Doc" when she met Dr. Bartner and members of the Trojan Marching Band.

A Forty Year Timeline

1970

The Trojan Marching Band uniforms as they were when Dr. Arthur C. Bartner arrived at USC.

JUN. 29 Dr. Arthur C. Bartner leaves his position as director of the Davison High School band in Michigan, taking a pay cut to become the director of the USC Trojan Marching Band.

SEP. 08 Starting with 50 members, Bartner organizes his first band camp at Idyllwild, California.

SEP. 19 At the first football game, USC vs. Nebraska in the Coliseum, the Trojan Marching Band's ranks have grown to 80 members. His inaugural halftime show is titled, Those Were the Days, and features the standards *Three O'Clock in the Morning* and *When the Moon Comes Over the Mountain* mixed with Broadway hits *Aquarius* and *Big Spender*. The game is a tie 21-21.

FALL Along with coach Marv Goux, Bartner revolutionizes the "Jock Rally" where the band and football team meet for a rally with speeches and songs on Friday afternoons before home game days. The first rally takes place in the basement of the Physical Education building.

OCT. 31 Phillip Diamon, the Senior Manager of the Cal Band after seeing the USC band perform at a game versus the Bears writes, "This was unquestionably the best Trojan Band we have seen."

NOV. 28 Composer Henry Mancini conducts the band at halftime of the Notre Dame game. The show features *March of the Cue Balls* from the television series, *Mr. Lucky,* and some of his other hits: *The Pink Panther Theme, Baby Elephant Walk* and *It Had Better Be Tonight.* Despite a steady downpour, the segment is filmed and used on his televised special *Monsanto Presents Mancini,* which airs the following April in 1971.

DEC. 10 The first Trojan Marching Band Banquet is held at the Blarney Castle in Los Angeles.

IN THE WORLD The Apollo 13 mission returns safely to Earth
U.S. troops invade Cambodia.
IBM introduces the floppy disk.
Monday Night Football debuts on ABC television.
The Beatles break up.

1971

The mellophone section of the Trojan Marching Band in 1971.

SPRING The "Helmet Club" is formed to finance the purchase of new uniforms. Contributors of $100 or more get an inscribed helmet and the latest recording of the fight songs. Dr. Milo Sweet – composer of *Fight On!* – is the first member.

FEB The band performs for the first time at Disneyland taking part in the I Am an American Ceremony in Town Square, celebrating the birthdays of Washington and Lincoln.

FEB. 27 The band gets one of its first showbiz gigs: a Beech-Nut commercial filmed at the Coliseum.

Tony Fox begins providing musical arrangements and soon becomes staff arranger, helping develop the distinctive sound of the band. Tony will eventually rise to the position of Associate Director and be involved in all aspects of the organization, including leadership of the Basketball Band.

FALL New, more comfortable uniforms designed by the Walt Disney Company and Robert Jani debut for the 1971 football season. The famous "moon boots" are part of the new outfit and a new Greek key design graces the tunic. Female band members are allowed to join the band for the first time since World War II and sixteen sign up. The band's color guard – the USC Silks – are also formed. 100 band members take the field for the season, up 25% from the year before.

SEP. 10 Meredith Willson, the composer of *The Music Man,* guest conducts the Trojan Marching Band and the massed bands at High School Band Day.

IN THE WORLD The Pentagon Papers are published by the *New York Times.*
All in the Family debuts on CBS television.
The first microprocessor is introduced by Intel.
The 26th Amendment lowers the legal voting age to 18.
Patton wins the Oscar for Best Picture.

1972

Louie Bellson with the band at a USC vs. Notre Dame game.

FALL   A new set of helmets debuts, replacing the single piece, painted headgear that had been in use since 1950. The new helmet has a new visor and adds ear guards, but most prominent is an actual brush crowning the helmet.

DEC. 02   Jazz drummer Louie Bellson is the first major musician to guest star with the band as part of its Salute to Big Band Drummers at halftime of the Notre Dame game. He performs his hit *Carnaby Street* (*photo above*).

DEC. 20   Dr. Milo Sweet writes to the Trojan Marching Band to say, "I'm sure that your music helped to put the Trojans in the Rose Bowl, believe it or not."

IN THE WORLD   President Nixon visits China.
The Watergate Scandal breaks in Washington, D.C.
Pong – the first video game – is released by Atari.
The first digital watches are sold.
The first pay cable network HBO debuts.

1973

(below) Dr. Arthur C. Bartner with Neil Diamond, and (right) with his two children and Diana Ross.

JAN. 01   Dr. Bartner takes the Trojan Marching Band to the Rose Parade and Rose Bowl for the first time. Diana Ross arrives by helicopter to perform with the band before a national television audience. She sings *Our Love is Here to Stay* from her recent motion picture, *Lady Sings the Blues.* The Trojans beat Ohio State 42-17 to claim the National Championship.

SEP. 28   Two thousand fans show up to watch the band perform at a rally in the underground Arco Plaza downtown before the Trojans - Oklahoma Sooners game at the Coliseum. The event is billed as the first USC football rally in downtown L.A. in 42 years.

OCT. 20   On the 50th Anniversary of the composing of USC's alma mater, *All Hail,* Al Wesson, the composer, and the first arranger, Frank Lanterman, are honored by the band at halftime of the Homecoming game against Oregon.

OCT. 27   The Trojan Marching Band performs for the first time at Notre Dame Stadium. 175 members make the trip on a $30,000 budget. The traditional Notre Dame crowd gives the band a three-minute standing ovation following its performance of the rock hit *Frankenstein* with the USC Song Girls dancing along at halftime. Chicagoans get a bonus when their Mayor Richard Daley invites the band to play a noon rally at the Civic Center.

NOV. 24   Neil Diamond, who composed the music, *Dear Father,* for the movie *Jonathan Livingston Seagull* appears with the band when they perform his music at halftime of the USC-UCLA game.

IN THE WORLD   Arab nations begin an oil embargo against the U.S.
The U.S. Supreme Court rules on Roe v. Wade.
The Sears Tower is completed.
Skylab, the first American space station, is launched.
The Godfather wins the Academy Award for Best Picture.

1974

JAN. 01   For the second consecutive year, the Trojan Marching Band goes to the Rose Bowl. Broadway singer and TV star John Davidson *(photo above left)* sings the National Anthem with them before the game, and at halftime, the popular funk band Tower of Power performs their hit *So Very Hard to Go.* The Trojans lose to Ohio State, 42-21.

          The city of Toluca, Mexico asks Dr. Bartner to form the first Mexican marching band program.

SUMMER   Dr. Bartner is named director of the All-American College Marching Band at Walt Disney World, beginning three decades of summer work for Disney. Musicians from colleges around the country audition for a chance to perform in the group for the summer season. He then ran the Disneyland version in 1975 and from 1977 to 2005.

NOV. 30   When the Trojans are down 24 points to top-ranked Notre Dame in the first half, the Trojan Marching Band keeps up the spirit. Tailback Anthony Davis makes a touchdown catch just before halftime and a 3rd quarter opening kickoff return for another. The Trojans, on their way to a National Championship, beat the stunned Irish 55-24. Before the game, Carol Lawrence sings the National Anthem with the band *(photo above right)*, and husband, Robert Goulet sings music from the motion picture *The Little Prince* at halftime.

NOV. 25   The Trojan Marching Band steps inside a television studio for the first time, taping a special Christmas *Dinah!* Dinah Shore hosts, interviewing Dr. Bartner. Another guest star, Rock Hudson, acting as drum major leads the band into the studio, where they play a number of Christmas carols.

DEC. 29   The *Los Angeles Times* publishes an article entitled *USC Band May be Trojans' Work Horse.*

IN THE WORLD   President Nixon resigns the presidency and is succeeded by Gerald Ford.
          Patty Hearst is kidnapped by the Symbionese Liberation Army.
          The national speed limit is set at 55 mph.
          People magazine debuts.
          Chinatown is released.

1975

(above) Dr. Bartner with his two children at the taping of Mitzi and 100 Guys.

(left) The Trojan Marching Band rehearses for the Liberty Bowl in Memphis, Tennessee.

JAN. 01   USC's 3rd Rose Bowl in three years is an 18-17 win over Ohio State to earn the Trojans the National Championship. The theme of the band's halftime show is entitled *Make Your Own Kind of Music* and features *Give It One* by Maynard Ferguson and *Dance to the Music* by Sly and the Family Stone.

MAR   The band's first recorded album, titled *The Spirit of Troy,* is released, and Includes some of the first numbers that established the band's modern sound, including *Give it One* and Elton John's *The Bitch is Back.* Also included on the album is the band's distinctive arrangement of *Stars and Stripes Rock,* which remains popular to this day.

MAR. 24   The Trojan Marching Band – wearing tuxedos, not uniforms – provides 75 of Mitzi Gaynor's men for her special *Mitzi and 100 Guys.* Bob Hope and Andy Griffith also star.

DEC   The band performs on film for the opening of MGM's *That's Entertainment, Part II* for release in 1976. Although it's their first motion picture appearance, the band with its numerous television gigs and famous guest stars, is fast becoming known as "Hollywood's Band."

DEC. 22   The Liberty Bowl in Memphis, Tennessee provides a new setting for the band to celebrate America's Bicentennial with an elaborate patriotic halftime show. The pregame performance includes renowned opera soprano Marguerite Piazza singing the national anthem with the Trojan Marching Band. USC trounces Texas A & M, 20-0. It's John McKay's last game as head coach. He is succeeded by John Robinson.

IN THE WORLD   The Vietnam war ends.
          Home videotape systems are introduced in Japan.
          Muhammad Ali beats Joe Frazier in the "Thrilla in Manila"
          Saturday Night Live debuts on NBC.
          A Chorus Line premieres on Broadway.

1976

MAR. 22 — The band appears on the Fifth Anniversary Special of KNBC's *Sunday Show* at Busch Gardens in Van Nuys, California.

MAR. 29 — After an introduction by Elizabeth Taylor and Gene Kelly, the Trojan Marching Band enters the Dorothy Chandler Pavilion from all the different doors and performs *America the Beautiful* during the finale of the 48th Annual Academy Awards with many Hollywood stars singing along. Famed Hollywood composer and conductor John Williams is musical director of the event.

OCT. 07 — The Trojan Marching Band performs for President Gerald Ford when he speaks on the steps of Doheny Library.

OCT. 23 — The Trojan Alumni Band *(photo above)* makes its first appearance at Homecoming.

NOV. 12 — The band's busy year in front of the camera continues with *Two-Minute Warning* in which they portray a marching band at the championship game. The film stars Charlton Heston.

NOV. 27 — Neil Sedaka sings *Love Will Keep Us Together* with the Trojan Marching Band during the halftime show of the USC-Notre Dame game.

DEC — In keeping with its growing showbiz resume, the band performs for the Hollywood premiere of *King Kong,* the remake of the 1933 classic.

IN THE WORLD — Jimmy Carter is elected President.
America celebrates its Bicentennial.
CB Radio popularity hits its peak.
NASA unveils the first space shuttle.
Alex Haley publishes *Roots.*

1977

JAN. 01 — The fourth Rose Bowl for the Trojan Marching Band under the direction of Dr. Arthur C. Bartner is a 14-6 win over his alma mater, the University of Michigan. The band's halftime show salutes Los Angeles: The Entertainment Capital of the World, performing *California Dreamin'* and *MacArthur Park.*

JAN. 08 — On the eve of Super Bowl XI, live from the Rose Bowl, the band appears on *Super Night at the Super Bowl, an* "all-star celebrity salute" hosted by Sammy Davis, Jr., Elliott Gould, and Andy Williams with Trojan alumnus John Wayne as a special guest *(photos above).*

SPRING — The second Trojan Marching Band album is released entitled *The Conquest Goes On....* The album features *Dance to the Music* by Sly and the Family Stone, which remains in the band's repertoire today.

MAY 19 — The band performs for Muhammad Ali at the ABC Entertainment Center in Century City for the premiere of his motion picture biography, *The Greatest.*

SEP. 30 — With the Silks wearing stormtrooper costumes and some of the band members dressed as the main characters of *Star Wars,* the Trojan Marching Band performs a special tribute to the blockbuster film at the halftime of the USC-Washington State game.

OCT. 16 — The band performs at Game 5 of the World Series matching the Dodgers against the Yankees at Dodger Stadium.

NOV. 07 — *Los Angeles Times* columnist John Hall, in his column The Sideshow "nominates" the band for the Heisman Trophy after seeing their halftime show at the USC-Stanford game.

NOV. 25 — Maynard Ferguson performs with the band for the first of many times, playing *Gonna Fly Now* from the motion picture *Rocky* at halftime of the UCLA game.

DEC. 31 — The band travels to Houston for the Bluebonnet Bowl in the Astrodome where the Trojans defeat Texas A&M 47-28. The halftime show features disco hits, *Boogie Nights* and *How Deep Is Your Love?*

IN THE WORLD — President Carter pardons Vietnam War draft evaders.
Red Dye No. 2 is banned.
Magnetic Resonance Imaging is first used on a human.
Saturday Night Fever sparks the disco craze.
Star Wars breaks records at the box office.

1978

Right:
Dr. Arthur C. Bartner with composer
Quincy Jones.

Left:

Dr. Bartner being interviewed in Japan by ESPN for the annual Japan Bowl.

JAN. 14 Dr. Bartner is chosen as musical director for the annual Japan Bowl – the American Collegiate All-Star Football Game – held in Tokyo, Japan. He holds the post until the Japan Bowl ceases operation in 1993.

JUN. 05 The Trojan Marching Band performs at Paramount Studios for the premiere of the soon-to-be hit movie musical, *Grease.*

SEP. 09 Comedian Steve Allen guest conducts the Trojan Marching Band at the annual High School Band Day.

OCT. 11 The Trojan Marching Band performs a pregame program at Dodger Stadium before Game 2 of the World Series.

NOV. 25 Producer Quincy Jones appears with the band for a special *The Wiz* halftime show featuring characters from the movie at the Notre Dame - USC game.

DEC. 02 The band travels to Hawaii for the first time and the Trojans beat the Rainbow Warriors, 21-5.

IN THE WORLD Pope John Paul II is elected to the Papacy.
The Camp David Accords are signed.
The first test-tube baby is born.
The comic strip *Garfield* debuts.

186

1979

Dr. Bartner with
Mick Fleetwood.

JAN. 1 The Trojan Marching Band sees a USC victory over the Michigan Wolverines 17-10 in their fifth Rose Bowl. The band's selections at halftime include the theme to the previous summer's hit *Animal House,* and John Williams' iconic theme from *Superman.*

A third album titled, *The Trojan Marching Band,* is released with two songs on the album – *Getaway and Fantasy* – that are hits from the popular funk group Earth, Wind, & Fire.

JUN. 16 At the invitation of Mick Fleetwood, the Trojan Marching Band records instrumental lines for the title track of the Fleetwood Mac album *Tusk* at Dodger Stadium. Footage from the recording session is released as a music video (one of the first in regular rotation when MTV debuts two years later). The album sells over a million copies and the Trojan Marching Band becomes the first collegiate marching band to earn a platinum album.

OCT. 10 The band plays *Fight On!* for the climactic scene of Chuck Barris' *Gong Show Movie* being filmed in Pismo Beach. It's the band's second motion picture.

OCT. 16 A brass, drum set, and bass ensemble made up of Trojan Marching Band members performs at the first Los Angeles Lakers home game of the season at the request of owner Jerry Buss. The group, now known as the Laker Band, has played at all Lakers home games for 30 years and counting.

DEC. 04 The Trojan Marching Band plays the first of five concerts with Fleetwood Mac at the Los Angeles Forum to rave reviews from the local press.

IN THE WORLD Ayatollah Khomeini leads the Islamic Revolution in Iran.
The Soviets invade Afghanistan.
Mother Teresa receives the Nobel Peace Prize.
The first commercial rap hit, *Rapper's Delight,* is released.
ESPN begins broadcasting.

1980

Dr. Bartner displaying the platinum album presented to the band by Fleetwood Mac.

JAN. 01   A 6th Rose Bowl with the Trojan Marching Band is a 17-16 win over the Buckeyes of Ohio State. The band performs their new hit *Tusk* at halftime, forming the letters TUSK on the field and morphing it into to TUSC.

JAN. 05   Introduced by Dionne Warwick and Glen Campbell, the Trojan Marching Band opens the music countdown television show *Solid Gold '79*, performing *Tusk* in studio while the song's music video is played.

Provost Cornelius Ping reorganizes the Trojan Marching Band's position within the university, giving Dr. Bartner more control over the band's administration and finances.

The band releases its 4th album, *The Trojan Marching Band, 1880-1980*. This album celebrates the university's centennial and features Trojan fight songs from throughout the century, including *Carry On, Cardinal and Gold,* and *Song of Troy*.

JUL. 08   Dr. Bartner directs a massed band for the pregame festivities of the 1980 Major League Baseball All-Star Game at Dodger Stadium.

OCT. 04   Commemorating the 100th Anniversary of USC's founding, new band uniforms debut at the Homecoming game versus Arizona State. The old "moon boots" are replaced by white spats and the band now wears white gauntlets. New jackets have a Trojan head on a shield, and pants have gold and white striping down the sides. Helmets have a soft visor, but still have brushes. At halftime of the game, members of Fleetwood Mac present Dr. Bartner with the platinum album from *Tusk*.

IN THE WORLD   Ronald Reagan is elected President.
The U.S. men's hockey team beats the Soviets in Lake Placid.
3M introduces Post-It Notes.
Who Shot J.R.? draws record television viewers.
PacMan is released.

1981

To Members of the U.S.C. Trojan Marching Band – With appreciation & admiration – Ronald Reagan

JAN. 13   The band performs for newly-elected President Ronald Reagan at Los Angeles City Hall as he departs for Washington, D.C. *(pictured above at his return to Los Angeles in 1989).*

APR. 03   At The Sports Imports Invitational at Ohio State University, the band plays at breaks during the tournament that features the four best men's volleyball teams in the nation (including the defending champion Trojans).

APR. 19   ABC television's *Omnibus* tapes a segment at the Rose Bowl featuring the Trojan Marching Band.

IN THE WORLD   Iran frees U.S. hostages.
The first female Supreme Court Justice Sandra Day O'Connor is sworn in.
The IBM PC is introduced.
Raiders of the Lost Ark is released.
MTV goes on the air.

1982

JAN. 01 The band follows the Trojans out to the Fiesta Bowl in Tempe, Arizona. The Trojans lose to Penn State, 26-10.

MAR. 07 The Trojan Marching Band's 5th album titled *The Spirit of Troy,* is released. It features some of the band's greatest "rock charts" including *China Grove, Heartbreaker, In the Stone*, and the band's first solo recording of *Tusk*.

APR. 06 Dr. Bartner directs a mass band of Los Angeles-area high schools for Opening Day of the Dodgers at Dodger Stadium. This becomes an annual tradition for over twenty years until the Dodgers organization ends the practice.

JUL. 04 The much-anticipated sequel to the hit movie musical *Grease* is released. The Trojan Marching Band portrays the Rydell High School Marching Band in *Grease II* *(photo above)*.

JUL. 04 The Trojan Marching Band performs for the first time at the Hollywood Bowl. The title of the sold-out concert is *Family Fireworks Picnic Concert* and features the band playing both USC standards and John Philip Sousa marches. Sesame Street's Big Bird is the special guest and even conducts the band.

SEP. 25 Because of the generosity of the band's supporters, Jim and Darlene Milligan, the entire Trojan Marching Band makes the trip to Norman, Oklahoma to see the team shutout the Sooners, 12-0.

OCT. 01 Dr. Bartner conducts the 450-piece All-American College Marching Band for the opening of EPCOT Center at Walt Disney World, Florida.

NOV. 23 John Robinson resigns as coach of USC football. Offensive coordinator Ted Tollner replaces him.

IN THE WORLD Great Britain overcomes Argentina in the Falklands War.
The Vietnam Veterans War Memorial Wall is dedicated.
The first artificial heart is implanted.
Michael Jackson's *Thriller* tops the album charts.
Cats opens on Broadway.

1983

Tommy Lasorda, Dr. Arthur C. Bartner, and Rod Dedeaux with Mike Nyeholt and Song Girls at the Swim with Mike *charity event in the 90's.*

APR. 03 The band follows Cheryl Miller and the Women of Troy basketball team to the National Championship in Norfolk, Virginia. It's the first of two titles for the team.

APR "Pops at Pickfair" is held as a gala event at the Hollywood home of the legendary film stars, Douglas Fairbanks and Mary Pickford, currently owned by the Lakers pro-basketball team owner, Jerry Buss. The Spirit of Troy support group is formed to raise scholarships for band members.

APR The band opens the McDonald's Swim Stadium on campus at a weekday ceremony then returns to the pool that Saturday for the 3rd Annual Swim With Mike charity event. This volunteer swim-a-thon benefits physically-disabled athletes in honor of Mike Nyeholt, a USC swimmer who was paralyzed in 1981. The band returns to perform for the event every year *(photo above)*.

OCT. 15 Over 200 Trojan Olympians from the preceding 80 years are honored by the Trojan Marching Band at halftime of the Homecoming game against Arizona.

NOV. 05 During the half-time show at the home game versus "The Farm," the Trojan Marching Band re-enacts "The Play" – which was an already famous last-second comeback win for Cal over Stanford the previous year. The Stanford Band attempts to disrupt the show by running into the end zone.

NOV. 06 After watching the Stanford game, Allan Malamud, a columnist for the *Los Angeles Herald Examiner,* writes that "...the best coaching job on campus this year again is being done by Dr. Arthur C. Bartner. Bartner may be the greatest band leader to grace Hollywood since Glenn Miller."

IN THE WORLD Sally Ride becomes the first American woman in space.
Just Say No is introduced as an anti-drug advertising campaign.
Cabbage Patch Kids dolls are introduced.
The final episode of *M*A*S*H* airs.
Alice Walker publishes *The Color Purple*.

1984

Dr. Bartner is celebrated by his students in Disney's All American College Marching Band, *a predecessor to the Olympic All American Marching Band.*

SPRING   As a prelude to the impending Summer Olympics, the Trojan Marching Band releases *Let the Games Begin* – the 6th album under the direction of Dr. Arthur C. Bartner. The album features Olympian music such as *Bugler's Dream, March of the Olympians,* and *America the Beautiful.*

JUL. 28   Dr. Bartner forms and conducts the 800-strong Olympic All-American Marching Band for the XXIII Olympiad in Los Angeles, performing at the opening and closing ceremonies of the 1984 Summer Olympic Games at the Coliseum. The band continues to perform throughout the games at various events, including the opening of the baseball exhibition. Smaller "venue bands" play at individual sports stadiums throughout the Games.

FALL   The band's drumline begins playing on Yamaha drums. The company continues as a sponsor to the present day.

OCT. 20   To celebrate the USC School of Music's 100th anniversary, David Wolper, Tommy Walker and Art Bartner are honored at halftime of the Homecoming game.

NOV. 24   Honoring his work for the Olympics, Dr. Arthur C. Bartner Day is declared in Los Angeles.

     Writer Jon Krampner dubs the Trojan Marching Band as "Hollywood's Band" in a magazine feature about Dr. Bartner's 15 years with the program. "... the Trojan Marching Band has acquired the unofficial title 'Band of the Stars.' If the Dallas Cowboys are America's Team, then this is Hollywood's Band."

IN THE WORLD   U.S. Marines withdraw from Beirut.
Ronald Reagan is reelected in a landslide.
The AIDS virus is discovered.
The Cosby Show debuts on NBC.
Bruce Springsteen's *Born in the U.S.A.* is released.

1985

Dr. Bartner's daughter Debbie (center) becomes a USC Song Girl as a junior. She wears the white sweater for two years.

JAN. 01   Dr. Arthur C. Bartner directs the Trojan Marching Band in his 7th Rose Bowl which turns out to be a victory over Ohio State, 20-17. The band performs a special Olympic-themed salute to America at halftime, featuring a funk version of Aaron Copland's *Fanfare for the Common Man*, John Williams' *Olympic Fanfare and Theme,* and a giant inflatable Statue of Liberty with 5,000 red, white, and blue balloons released into the sky.

JAN. 20   Dr. Bartner directs the All-American College Marching Band in Washington, D.C. for the 50th American Presidential Inauguration (Ronald Reagan). The Inaugural Parade is canceled due to the extreme cold but the band still performs a concert in the Capital Centre.

FEB. 18   The Trojan Marching Band is part of an all-star cast for the *Disneyland 30th Anniversary Celebration* that airs nationwide on NBC. Tony Fox is nominated for an Emmy for his work arranging the music for the special.

NOV. 30   In its first international trip, the Trojan Marching Band goes to Tokyo for the Mirage Bowl regular season match-up of USC versus the Oregon Ducks.

AUG. 29   Breaking the record for the largest marching band ever assembled, Dr. Bartner takes the lead of 5,000 high school band members for the reopening of Union Station in St. Louis.

OCT. 05   Danny Kaye is a guest conductor during halftime of the Homecoming game versus the Oregon State Beavers.

DEC. 28   The band travels to Hawai'i for the Aloha Bowl. The Trojans lose to Alabama 24-3.

IN THE WORLD   Mikhail Gorbachev becomes leader of the U.S.S.R.
The Antarctic hole in the Earth's ozone layer is discovered.
The wreck of the Titanic is located.
We Are the World is released.
The Nintendo Entertainment System debuts.

1986

JUL. 03 Dr. Bartner directs the 500-piece All-American College Marching Band for the Opening Ceremonies of Liberty Weekend in New York to celebrate the rededication of the Statue of Liberty. The Trojan Marching Band drumline is a part of the group and plays at a special ceremony with President Reagan onboard an aircraft carrier on July 4. The Liberty Band also plays for the Closing Ceremonies on July 5 at the Meadowlands

JUL. 25 Dr. Bartner directs a 400-piece massed band for the Opening Ceremonies of the U.S. Olympic Festival in Houston, Texas *(photo above)*.

SUMMER The TMB travels to Lake Tahoe for the USC Alumni Club of Northern Nevada's SCend-Off of incoming Trojan freshmen beginning an annual summer tradition that lasts to this day.

NOV The band performs at "Up the Irish," a party thrown at Trojan Marching Band friends Ken and Barbara Cotler's house as a pre-Notre Dame game rally. The band continues to perform at the event – which is held every other year when the Trojans host the game – until the present day. It's grown so popular it now takes place in Bovard Auditorium.

NOV. 29 The Trojan Marching Band debuts its newest set of uniforms in a big way at the Notre Dame game. After wearing its old ones for the first two quarters, the band marches down the Peristyle at halftime in their new set. It is an updated version of the previous set with inspiration drawn from the uniforms of the Olympic All-American Marching Band. It has a larger white shield on the front with the Trojan head logo on it. The gauntlets are discarded and a new, longer cape debuts. The Greek Key design is removed and the cape is now tapered with yellow on the backside and white inside. The band uses the uniform for 14 years.

IN THE WORLD President Reagan orders air strikes against Libya.
The Iran Contra Scandal breaks.
Voyager makes the first nonstop flight around the world without refueling.
Halley's Comet passes by Earth.
The Oprah Winfrey Show debuts nationally.

1987

JAN. 01 The Trojan Marching Band makes its first trip to the Citrus Bowl in Orlando, Florida. In Ted Tollner's last game as coach, the Trojans lose 16-7 to Auburn.

JAN. 25 The band participates in the halftime show of Super Bowl XXI, *Salute to Hollywood's 100th Anniversary*, with Mickey Rooney and George Burns at the Rose Bowl.

MAR. 02 The Trojan Marching Band appears in the *Can't Cry Anymore* video for the rock group Kansas. The video airs on MTV.

AUG. 08 Billed as the largest outdoor live entertainment show held in the United States, Dr. Bartner leads a 1,000-piece massed band at the Tenth Pan American Games Opening Ceremony at the Indianapolis Motor Speedway *(photo above)*.

SEP. 16 Fanfare trumpets from the Trojan Marching Band perform for Pope John Paul II's mass at Dodger Stadium.

SEP. 17 The Official Fanfare Unit, under the direction of Dr. Arthur C. Bartner, leads a parade from Independence Hall to the Philadelphia Museum of Art as part of *We the People 200*, a celebration of the 200th Anniversary of the Constitution.

SEP. 18 The movie, *Amazon Women on the Moon*, premieres with the Trojan Marching Band playing the role of a marching band in the Titan Man segment.

SEP. 19 First year coach Larry Smith requests that the Trojan Marching Band never miss a game – home or away. In the 23 years since, the band has been to over 280 consecutive games.

DEC The Trojan Marching Band records its 8th album, *Spirit of Troy Live and in Concert*. The LP is recorded in front of a live audience in the Coliseum and replicates the pregame, halftime, and postgame shows at the upcoming Rose Bowl. Included on the album are rock chart standards *Tequila; Louie, Louie;* and *La Bamba*.

IN THE WORLD Margaret Thatcher is elected for a third term as British Prime Minister.
Baby Jessica is rescued from a Texas well after 3 days.
The anti-depressant drug Prozac is approved for use by the FDA.
The Simpsons debuts on *The Tracey Ullman Show*.
Toni Morrison's *Beloved* is published.

1988

Dr. Arthur C. Bartner greets the Duke and Duchess of York with Mayor and Mrs. Tom Bradley.

JAN. 02 The Trojan Marching Band's 8th Rose Bowl program at halftime include the Buddy Rich jazz classic *Channel One Suite* and the recent hit from the *Beverly Hills Cop II* soundtrack, *Shakedown*. The Michigan State Spartans won the game.

JAN. 31 Dr. Bartner leads a massed band, which includes the Trojan Marching Band, for the halftime show of Super Bowl XXII entitled "Something Grand" at Jack Murphy Stadium in San Diego, featuring Chubby Checker and the Rockettes.

FEB. 27 The Trojan Marching Band welcomes the Duke and Duchess of York to Los Angeles at a ceremony held at City Hall.

MAY The Trojan Marching Band travels to Australia, beginning a tradition of biennial international goodwill tours. On the occasion of the country's bicentenary, the band tours Sydney, performs in Darling Harbour, plays for a North Sydney Bears rugby match, then finishes the trip with a performance at the 1988 World Expo in Brisbane.

JUL. 21 Dr. Bartner leads a massed band for the closing day of the Democratic National Convention in Atlanta, Georgia.

FALL New, sturdier helmets debut with longer ear plates and a larger, redesigned visor, and continue to be used today.

OCT. 15 Film composer Bruce Broughton conducts the Trojan Marching Band combined with local bands for High School Band Day. The massed band plays a collection of his pieces including the theme to the movie *Silverado*.

OCT. 16 The Trojan Marching Band performs at Dodger Stadium before Game 2 of the World Series.

DEC. 02 The Trojan Marching Band appears with Leslie Nielsen and George Kennedy in the climactic scene of *The Naked Gun: From the Files of Police Squad!*

IN THE WORLD The Soviet Union withdraws from Afghanistan
George H. W. Bush is elected President.
CD's outsell vinyl records for the first time ever.
Bobby McFerrin releases *Don't Worry, Be Happy*.
The Phantom of the Opera opens on Broadway.

1989

Left: Garry Marshall and publicity director of Paramount Studios Hank Ehrlich with the band for the opening of their New York street.

JAN. 02 The Trojan Marching Band makes its 9th appearance in the Rose Bowl, performing a special big band version of the *Countermarch* at halftime, and honoring the 100th anniversary of the Tournament of Roses, the band spells out "So Cal" on the field.

JAN. 05 The Trojan Marching Band records 36 college fight songs at Bovard Auditorium that are released as a CD and cassette.

JAN. 20 The Trojan Marching Band performs at Los Angeles International Airport as President Ronald Reagan and the first lady return to California following his term in the White House. A band member gives his helmet to the President who wears it proudly for press photographers *(photo on page 187)*.

APR. 30 The Trojan Marching Band presents a "Pops at Paramount" concert at Paramount Studios. The USC Symphonic Brass Ensemble performs for the guests as well.

NOV. 04 The Trojan Marching Band performs with *Tonight Show* bandleader Doc Severinsen at halftime of the Oregon State game. He is made an honorary member of the band *(photo above right)*.

DEC. 06 The Trojan Marching Band performs *Happy Birthday* for the 25th Anniversary of the Los Angeles Music Center. Charlton Heston and Carol Channing are part of the festivities.

IN THE WORLD The Chinese government cracks down on protestors in Tiananmen Square.
The Exxon Valdez strikes a reef in Alaska.
A powerful earthquake strikes San Francisco during the World Series.

1990

Jan. 01   The Trojan Marching Band goes to the Rose Bowl for the tenth time under the direction of Dr. Arthur C. Bartner. Broadway and R&B singer Jennifer Holliday *(photo above)* performs *Auld Lang Syne* with the band at halftime. The Trojans defeat the Michigan Wolverines 17-10.

Jan. 25   The band appears on an episode of *L.A. Law* entitled "True Brit" *(photo above right).*

Jan. 28   Dr. Bartner directs a mass band for the halftime show of Super Bowl XXIV at the Louisiana Superdome in New Orleans. The halftime show is a salute to both New Orleans and the 40th anniversary of the comic strip *Peanuts*. The finale features a riverboat float that rises several stories high.

Apr. 22   To celebrate Dr. Bartner's 20 years with the program, the TMB presents a "Pops at the Police Academy" concert. Ken Dye hosts the event and the new Arthur C. Bartner Endowment is unveiled by President Zumberge to provide "Band Grants" for TMB members.

Jul. 04   The TMB makes its first appearance on Catalina Island for Avalon's Independence Day festivities at the invitation of USC Alumnus Dr. Jack Wall, beginning a tradition that lasts until the present day. The band marches in a parade at noon, performs a concert in the town plaza, then plays to a packed house at night in the world-famous Casino.

Jul. 06   Dr. Bartner leads a massed band for the opening ceremonies of the U.S. Olympic Festival at the Metrodome in Minneapolis, Minnesota.

Jul. 19   The Trojan Marching Band helps dedicate the Richard Nixon Presidential Library & Birthplace in Yorba Linda, CA. Current President George H.W. Bush and former Presidents Gerald Ford and Ronald Reagan join Nixon for the gala event.

Jul. 21   Dr. Bartner leads a massed band for the welcoming ceremony of the Goodwill Games at Husky Stadium in Seattle, Washington.

Jul–Aug   The Trojan Marching Band embarks on its second biennial international tour, visiting Europe for the reunification of Germany, playing at the Brandenburg Gate and on both sides of the Berlin Wall. The band also performs in the Netherlands, Belgium, Austria, and Italy during the 19 day trip.

Dec. 21   The Trojan Marching Band performs for the Golden Jubilee of the Pasadena Arroyo Seco Freeway.

Dec. 31   The Trojan Marching Band's second bowl game of the year is the John Hancock Bowl in El Paso, Texas. Band members see a bullfight in Juarez, Mexico then the Trojans lose to the Michigan State Spartans 17-16.

In the World   The South African government frees Nelson Mandela
General Manuel Noriega surrenders in Panama.
The Hubble Space Telescope is launched into orbit.
The NC-17 MPAA rating debuts.
Milli Vanilli admits to lip-synching its songs.

1991

FEB. 02   The Trojan Marching Band performs the theme song for *America's Funniest Home Video*s on the show's second season finale.

FEB. 06   The Trojan Marching Band performs for Ronald Reagan's 80th birthday party at the Beverly Hilton.

APR   The Trojan Marching Band appears on MTV's *Rock 'n Jock Diamond Derby*, which is shot on USC's Dedeaux Field.

APR. 21   The band records its first CD *Digital Trojan Band at Bovard Auditorium*. It features 25 tracks and includes all the band favorites from *In the Stone* to *Tusk* and newer hits like *Birdland, Get On Your Feet,* and *Hip to Be Square.*

APR. 28   The band presents a "Presidential Pops" concert at the Richard M. Nixon Library in Yorba Linda, California.

MAY. 01   The band helps Doogie ask Wanda to the prom on an episode of *Doogie Howser, M.D.*

JUL. 12   Dr. Bartner leads members of the Trojan Marching Band and a massed band of high schools for the Opening Ceremonies for the U.S. Olympic Festival at Dodger Stadium.

SEP. 30   The band helps Liza Minnelli unveil her star on the Hollywood Walk of Fame *(photo above right)*.

NOV. 09   The band salutes the cast of the original *Star Trek* series *(photo below right)* – including left to right: Dr. Bartner, James Doohan, George Takei, Walter Koenig, DeForest Kelley, and Leonard Nimoy – at halftime of the Washington game. The band performs the *Star Trek* theme in celebration the 25th anniversary of the show's premiere and to promote the release of *Star Trek VI: The Undiscovered Country.*

DEC. 13   The Bruce Willis action movie *The Last Boy Scout* premieres with the Trojan Marching Band portraying a marching band at a football game in the movie, filmed in the Coliseum.

DEC. 14   The TMB performs for the 200th Anniversary Celebration of the Bill of Rights at Los Angeles City Hall.

IN THE WORLD   A U.S. led coalition wins the Persian Gulf War.
                   The Soviet Union collapses.
                   Magic Johnson announces he tested positive for HIV.
                   Rock band Nirvana begins grunge movement.
                   Terminator II: Judgment Day debuts at box office.

1992

Mar	Dr. Bartner helps form the Royal Dutch Marching Band for the newly-opened Huis Ten Bosch theme park in Nagasaki, Japan.
Apr. 12	Dr. Bartner and Trojan Marching Band staff lead a massed band of American high schools for the opening of Euro Disneyland in France.
May	The band performs for the United States National Day on May 17 at Expo '92 in Seville, Spain—the second World Expo for the band and Dr. Bartner. The Vice President's wife Marilyn Quayle is the honored guest. The band also tours Madrid and makes a day trip to Morocco.
Jul. 13	Dr. Bartner leads a massed band for the opening of the Democratic National Convention at Madison Square Garden in New York.
Sep. 05	At the opening football game of the season versus San Diego State at Jack Murphy Stadium, Dr. Bartner tackles one of two Aztec fans who run on the field and attack drum major Bijon Watson.
Oct. 18	The Trojan Marching Band plays the opening ceremonies of the Los Angeles Inner-City Games. The band meets Arnold Schwarzenegger and Arsenio Hall *(photo above right)*.
Dec. 29	Operatic tenor and *Phantom of the Opera* star Davis Gaines performs with the Trojan Marching Band at the Freedom Bowl in Anaheim *(photo above left)*.
In the World	Presidents Yeltsin and Bush declare an end to the Cold War. The NAFTA treaty is signed. Bill Clinton is elected president. The Mall of America opens in Minnesota. Johnny Carson hosts *The Tonight Show* for last time.

1993

Jan. 31	The Trojan Marching Band participates in Michael Jackson's *Heal the World* halftime show at the Rose Bowl in Pasadena for Super Bowl XXVII.
Jun. 30	The Trojan Marching Band performs *Don't Let the Parade Pass You By* at Jerry Herman's Broadway at the Hollywood Bowl, a gala concert honoring the acclaimed composer of *Hello Dolly*. The concert is filmed and released later as a special on PBS.
Aug. 29	The band performs at the Disneyland Pigskin Classic in Anaheim to kickoff the Trojans' football season. KLOS radio deejays Mark & Brian are part of the band's halftime show devoted to Elvis Presley *(photo above)*. It's John Robinson's first game as a returning head coach.
Oct. 03	The band helps celebrate the reopening of the Los Angeles Central Library.
Oct. 14	The band plays as Governor Pete Wilson cuts a string of yellow silk poppies to officially open the 105 Freeway.
Nov. 17	The band performs for the opening ceremony of the Los Angeles Convention Center's South Hall.
Dec. 30	The Trojan Marching Band visits the Freedom Bowl for the second straight year, as the team wins over Utah 28-21.
In the World	Czechoslovakia splits into Slovakia and the Czech Republic. President Clinton introduces the military's "Don't Ask, Don't Tell" policy Singer Prince changes his name to a symbol. *Cheers* airs its final episode. *Mighty Morphin Power Rangers* debuts on television.

1994

FEB	The Trojan Marching Band performs for the reopening of Pershing Square in downtown Los Angeles.
MAR. 04	The band makes an appearance on *The Arsenio Hall Show*.
MAY	On its 4th biennial tour, the Trojan Marching Band goes to France and plays a concert under the Eiffel Tower. Other trip highlights include a visit to Normandy beach on the eve of the 50th Anniversary of D-Day and a performance at the famous church Sainte-Mère-Église.
JUL. 06	The Trojan Marching Band portrays the University of Alabama Marching Band circa 1960 in the film *Forrest Gump*. In the film, as Forrest Gump runs toward the band, the members stop him and even throw up a decidedly Trojan "V" for victory. The film went on to win six Oscars, including Best Picture.
JUN. 18	The Trojan Marching Band and local high school students comprise the World Cup Fanfare Unit under the direction of Dr. Bartner for the opening ceremonies of the soccer tournament at the Rose Bowl.
JUL. 16	The band plays during the intermission of *Encore – The Three Tenors*, the wildly popular concert featuring opera megastars Plácido Domingo, Luciano Pavarotti, and José Carerras at Dodger Stadium *(photo above)*.
AUG. 05	The band appears in *The Little Rascals*, the cinematic remake of the Depression-era *Our Gang* short films.
SEP	While back east for the game against Penn State, the band is honored on the floor of Congress by Congressman (and Trojan alum) Christopher Cox.
SEP. 24	Composer Alan Silvestri conducts the Trojan Marching Band and local bands for High School Band Day. The combined bands perform music from *Forrest Gump*.
OCT. 22	During a 61-0 Homecoming game drubbing of Cal, the Trojan Marching Band inaugurates the "Year of the Band" at halftime, officially beginning the celebration of Dr. Bartner's 25 years at USC.
FALL	The band releases *A Silver Celebration*, its 2nd CD and the 10th album under Dr. Bartner's direction. The CD is part of the "Year of the Band" celebration and features highlights from the first nine albums and newly recorded material that includes *Johnny's Mambo* and *Get It On*.
NOV. 27	The band kicks-off the 63rd Annual Hollywood Christmas Parade as part of the "Year of the Band" celebration with *Hooray for Hollywood*.
IN THE WORLD	The "Chunnel" connecting England and France opens. The World Series is canceled due to a strike. Figure skater Nancy Kerrigan is attacked. Steven Spielberg wins his first directing Oscar for *Schindler's List*. *Friends* debuts on NBC.

1995

Traveler leads the USC Trojans onto the field along with the Song Girls at the Cotton Bowl.

JAN. 02	The Trojan Marching Band travels south to Dallas, Texas for its first appearance at the Cotton Bowl. The Trojans decimate the Texas Tech Red Raiders 55-14.
SPRING	The Trojan Marching Band's first book is released in celebration of the "Year of the Band." It chronicles Dr. Arthur C. Bartner's 25 years at USC. It's illustrated with watercolors by Robert W. Jensen and written by Keith H. Walker.
APR. 29	The "Year of the Band" peaks with the elegant Silver Celebration Gala on the floor of the Coliseum hosted by *Star Trek: The Next Generation* star LeVar Burton. The show features special video tributes, guest speakers, and performances by Otis Day, Bill Conti, Louie Bellson, Mick Fleetwood, and *Phantom of the Opera* star Dale Kristien. It ends with a full band performance and a fireworks display over the Peristyle.
SEP. 08	The Juliette "Julie" Kohl Trojan Band Center opens in the basement of Stonier Hall across campus from the band's old cramped offices in Booth Hall. The band's new headquarters features offices for staff, a library, storage areas, and a student lounge.
OCT. 07	The 100th consecutive USC Football game with the Trojan Marching Band is a 26-16 win for the Trojans at Cal.
NOV. 04	The "Year of the Band" officially ends with a 750-strong alumni band joining the current 250 member band on the field for halftime of the Homecoming game. The combined bands form the largest letters ever on the field at the Coliseum.
IN THE WORLD	The U.S. space shuttle Atlantis docks with Russian space station Mir. O. J. Simpson is found not guilty. Microsoft releases Windows 95. Pierce Brosnan debuts as James Bond in *GoldenEye*. The WB and UPN television networks debut.

1996

JAN. 01 The Trojans' first Rose Bowl since 1990 is a win: 41-32 over Northwestern. The band's halftime show features the Weather Report hit *Birdland* and *The Blues Brothers*.

JAN. 18 The Trojan Marching Band performs for the gala premiere of *Mr. Holland's Opus* at the Cinerama Dome in Hollywood.

MAR. 29 The band appears as a military band in *Sgt. Bilko*, a remake of the 1950's sitcom *The Phil Silvers Show*. Steve Martin stars in the film.

APR. 27 The band kicks-off the Olympic torch relay at the Coliseum for its 84-day trek across the U.S. to Atlanta for the Centennial Games.

MAY On its 5th biennial international trip, the band braves English bad weather to perform at London's Hyde Park and inside Edinburgh Castle *(photo above on one of the good days)*.

OCT. 01 Dr. Bartner leads a massed band of 1,076 high school musicians for the 25th Anniversary of Walt Disney World in Florida.

NOV. 02 At halftime of the Homecoming game against Washington, the Trojan Marching Band honors alumnus and former drum major Larry Harmon, who went on to fame as Bozo the Clown.

NOV. 30 The Trojans break a string of 13 victories by Notre Dame with a 27-20 upset win over the Irish. At halftime, the band promotes the upcoming *Beavis and Butt-head Do America* by performing the movie's theme song with scenes from the film playing on the Coliseum's video board.

IN THE WORLD President Clinton is reelected in a landslide.
"Mad Cow" Disease breaks out in Great Britain.
The Unabomber is arrested.
Deep Blue computer defeats Garry Kasparov in chess.
Independence Day scores big at the box office.

1997

APR. 20 The USC Concert Band and Trojan Marching Band present the first Pops in Cerritos concert at the Cerritos Center for the Performing Arts beginning an annual tradition. Guest stars are band alumni that have successful professional music careers including composer Mark Watters and instrumentalists Richard Todd and Dave Washburn. Grammy-winning producer and arranger David Foster guest conducts the band.

MAY. 22 The Trojan Marching Band joins with Fleetwood Mac for a live reunion concert that is recorded over two days at Warner Bros Studios. The band performs an updated version of *Tusk* and closes the show with *Don't Stop*. The concert is released as a DVD and CD, entitled *The Dance*, which sells over five million copies in the U.S. alone. It's the Trojan Marching Band's second platinum album *(photo above)*.

NOV. 02 The Trojan Marching Band honors Chinese President Jiang Zemin with the Chinese National Anthem at a luncheon honoring him at the Beverly Hilton Hotel.

DEC. 17 Paul Hackett replaces John Robinson as head coach of the Trojans.

IN THE WORLD Hong Kong returns to Chinese rule.
The Mars Pathfinder lands on the Red Planet.
Titanic becomes the highest-grossing film in cinematic history.
The first *Harry Potter* book is published in Great Britain.
The television ratings system debuts.

1998

The Trojan Marching Band parades through Lisbon's World Expo '98.

JAN. 31   The Trojan Marching Band performs for the opening of the California Science Center at Exposition Park. Vice President Al Gore is among the guests.

MAY   Once again performing at a World Expo the band takes its second trip to the Iberian Peninsula in six years, this time, it's for Lisbon's Expo '98. Two days of performances in Lisbon, including the opening ceremonies for the U.S. Pavilion, cap the itinerary which includes Madrid, Toledo and Evora.

APR. 19   The second *Pops in Cerritos* concert features guest stars Charlie Bisharat, Louie Bellson, and composer Michael Kamen, who conducts the Trojan Marching Band and the Concert Band for *An American Symphony*, from the movie *Mr. Holland's Opus*.

OCT. 03   Michael Kamen conducts the Trojan Marching Band and local high school bands for the annual High School Band Day. The combined bands perform music from Kamen's scores for *Robin Hood: Prince of Thieves* and *Mr. Holland's Opus*.

NOV. 01   The Trojan Marching Band performs the national anthem before NASCAR's California 500 at Irwindale Speedway.

NOV. 28   At halftime of the Notre Dame game, Mick Fleetwood presents Dr. Bartner with the platinum album earned from the band's participation in *The Dance* album.

DEC. 06   The Trojan Marching Band support the men's water polo team as the Trojans beat Stanford 9-8 and win their first National Championship in Corona Del Mar.

DEC. 31   The band spends its New Year's Eve in El Paso, Texas for the Sun Bowl. The Trojans lose to TCU 28-19.

IN THE WORLD   The Good Friday Accord is reached in Northern Ireland.
President Clinton admits to having an affair with Monica Lewinksy.
The International Space Station is launched.
The Petronas Twin Towers in Kuala Lumpur are completed.
Seinfeld airs its final episode.

1999

Dr. Bartner with Latin jazz percussionist Poncho Sanchez at the Louisiana Tech game.

APR. 18   The band's third *Pops in Cerritos* features composer Elmer Bernstein as the guest conductor. The USC Concert Band performs music from his movie scores including *The Magnificent Seven* and *The Ten Commandments*.

NOV. 26   The Trojan Marching Band performs with Latin jazz percussionist Poncho Sanchez at halftime of the Louisiana Tech game.

FALL   The Trojan Marching Band releases its 11th album under the direction of Dr. Arthur C. Bartner titled *Spirit of Troy In Studio*. Most of the CD is recorded on Paramount Studios' Stage M and features a "pep/basketball band" sound, complete with rhythm section (electric bass, drumset, and latin percussion). Some new songs released on the album include *Tower of Power Medley* and *La Copa de la Vida*.

DEC. 31   The band performs downtown in the pouring rain as part of the Los Angeles Millennium Celebration.

DEC. 31   Dr. Bartner leads a massed band of high school musicians for America's Millennium Gala on the National Mall.

IN THE WORLD   President Clinton is impeached and acquitted.
The world fears the Y2K bug catastrophe.
The U.S. Women's Soccer team wins World Cup.
Woodstock '99 is held in New York.
The Pokémon craze peaks in the U.S.

2000

MAR. 26   Trojan Marching Band members are part of Robin Williams' *Blame Canada* musical segment of the 72nd Annual Academy Awards broadcast from the Shrine Auditorium.

APR   The band performs at intermissions of the Davis Cup tennis tournament pitting the USA versus the Czech Republic at the Great Western Forum.

APR. 16   The fourth Pops in Cerritos concert is entitled *Conquest! A Salute to Alfred Newman and His Film Legacy.* Preeminent Hollywood composers Elmer Bernstein, Basil Poledouris, Buddy Baker, Maria Newman, and Tommy Newman guest conduct the Concert Band in tribute to the celebrated film composer, who wrote the Trojan Marching Band's victory march *Conquest!* in 1947.

MAY   The band travels to Australia for the second time on its seventh biennial international tour visiting Oz on the eve of the Sydney Summer Olympic Games. The band also appears on two Australian television shows *(photo above left)* and at a Sydney Swans Australian Rules Football match. Another performance on the steps of the Sydney Opera House honors the U.S. Ambassador to Australia Genta Holmes, before traveling to Cairns in the northwest to visit the Great Barrier Reef.

JUN. 21   The Laker Band (made up of members of the Trojan Marching Band) is part of the Lakers' championship parade through Los Angeles that attracts nearly a quarter million people to Figueroa Street. The band rides atop a fire truck then plays on a stage in front of the Staples Center *(photo above right with the championship trophy).*

JUN. 23   At an opening night gala the Trojan Marching Band plays *Olympic Fanfare and Theme* for the induction of John Williams into the Hollywood Bowl Hall of Fame.

AUG. 14   The Trojan Marching Band is part of a massed band of local high school musicians directed by Dr. Bartner for the opening of the 2000 Democratic National Convention at the Staples Center.

AUG. 27   The Kickoff Classic in East Rutherford, New Jersey sees the debut of the band's first new uniforms in 14 years. The Trojans beat the Penn State Nittany Lions on national television, 29-5. Pete Carroll, who watches the game from the sidelines, is impressed with the Trojan Marching Band, according to a friend, who added, "He couldn't stop talking about the USC band. He said, 'You know, they don't have marching bands in the NFL'."

SEP. 02   The Trojan Marching Band works on Labor Day, performing on the *Jerry Lewis MDA Telethon.*

SEP. 23   The band performs for the world premiere of the motion picture *Remember the Titans* at the Rose Bowl.

OCT. 29   Dr. Bartner is profiled in a candid article in *Los Angeles Times Magazine* entitled "Trojan Hoarse; With a Demon's Voice and a God Complex, USC Band Director Art Bartner Has Built a Legend."

DEC. 15   Pete Carroll is hired as head coach of USC Football.

IN THE WORLD   Slobodan Milosevic is overthrown as President of Yugoslavia.
George W. Bush is elected President after Supreme Court ruling.
Sony launches the Playstation 2 video game system.
The Time Warner Inc. merger with AOL is the largest ever.
CSI: Crime Scene Investigation debuts on CBS.

2001

Composers Richard and Robert Sherman being made honorary band members at the Cerritos Pops Concert.

A Letter from Richard M. Sherman

Dr. Art Bartner is a joy to watch as he conducts his musical aggregations. His expertise, precision, and demand for excellence, is only surpassed by the inspiration and encouragement he imparts to his youthful musicians. It is no wonder that the USC Band has been rated one of the finest musical organizations in the nation for the past four decades.

FEB. 11   The Trojan Marching Band cheers on the Stars and Pros at MTV's *Rock and Jock BaseBrawl*, which is filmed at Cal State Fullerton

APR. 16   The docudrama *When Billie Beat Bobby* is released on ABC television. The Trojan Marching Band portrays the University of Texas Longhorn Marching Band in the recreation of the famous 1973 *Battle of the Sexes* tennis match.

APR. 29   The Trojan Marching Band's fifth *Pops in Cerritos* concert is entitled *Spirit of America*. It features guest conductor Richard Sherman, who leads the Concert Band in a medley of music that he and his brother Robert composed for Walt Disney. Both brothers are made honorary members of the Trojan Marching Band.

NOV. 30   The band honors film director and USC alumnus Robert Zemeckis at High School Band Day. The combined bands play music from his movies *Back to the Future* and *Forrest Gump*.

DEC. 25   The band performs at a bowl game on Christmas for the first time at the Las Vegas Bowl. The band stays at the Hard Rock Hotel and performs at a rally on Fremont Street. The Trojans lose to the Utah Utes 10-6.

IN THE WORLD   Ariel Sharon is elected prime minister of Israel.
U.S. declares war on the Taliban and Al Qaeda.
The first Apple iPod is released.
Tiger Woods becomes the first golfer to hold all four Majors titles.
The Lord of the Rings: The Fellowship of the Ring debuts.

Film maker and USC alum Robert Zemeckis with Dr. Bartner.

2002

Dr. Bartner,
Congrats on forty years at the helm of the greatest marching band in the history of the universe. As an alumnus, I'm especially proud of the marching band's achievements during your tenure and grateful to have had the opportunity for The Offspring and the Trojan Marching Band to collaborate together.

Fight On! Rock On!

Dexter Holland, The Offspring

JAN. 15	The Trojan Marching Band welcomes the Olympic Torch to the Coliseum on its way to Salt Lake City for the Winter Olympic Games.
APR. 26	The band joins Mayor Richard Riordan for the rededication of Los Angeles City Hall on its 74th Anniversary.
APR. 28	The Trojan Marching Band presents *America the Beautiful*, its sixth *Pops in Cerritos* concert. Special guest performers include singer Barbara Morrison (back for her second year) and the St. Charles Borromeo Choir conducted by Paul Salamunovich.
MAY	The Trojan Marching Band embarks on a "Three Capitals Tour" through the Eastern European cities of Budapest, Vienna, and Prague. The TMB performs a concert in each city. While preparing for its set in Prague, U.S. Secret Service agents protecting First Lady Laura Bush on her solo European tour overhear the band warming up. The TMB is subsequently invited to perform the next day at the U.S. Ambassador's residence for a reception honoring Mrs. Bush.
OCT. 19	The band honors The Offspring lead singer and USC alumnus Dexter Holland at the Washington game *(photo above)*, playing three hits from the group at halftime. Dexter is made an honorary member of the Trojan Marching Band.
DEC. 01	The Trojan Marching Band marches in the nationally-televised *Hollywood Christmas Parade* temporarily renamed the *Blockbuster Hollywood Christmas Spectacular*.
DEC. 21	The band goes to New Orleans for the NCAA Division Championship where the Women of Troy Volleyball team beats Stanford 3-1 for the first of two consecutive titles.
IN THE WORLD	The Department of Homeland Security is created. The Enron downfall leads a spate of corporate scandals. The Lakers win the last of three consecutive NBA championships. Halle Berry is the first African American to win a Best Actress Oscar. *American Idol: The Search for a Superstar* debuts.

2003

JAN. 02	The Trojan Marching Band travels to Miami for the FedEx Orange Bowl, its first Bowl Championship Series game. Heisman Trophy-winner Carson Palmer leads the Trojans to a 38-17 victory over the Iowa Hawkeyes.
FEB. 04	The band performs at the Cathay Pacific International New Year's Parade in Hong Kong. The band is only the second American group (behind the Dallas Cowboy Cheerleaders) to be invited to perform in the parade, which is broadcast to millions on television throughout Asia. The Trojan Marching Band also performs on top of Hong Kong's tallest mountain, Victoria Peak.
JAN. 19	The band tapes an episode of *Hollywood Squares* for the College Tournament Finals *(photo above)*.
MAR. 09	The Trojan Marching Band records college fight songs at Paramount Studios for the 989 Sports video game *NCAA GameBreaker 2004*.
APR. 13	The seventh *Pops in Cerritos* concert is entitled *The Spirit of Troy on Broadway*. Special guest stars for this showcase of hits from the Great White Way include Patti Austin, Dale Kristien, and television star Sharon Gless.
AUG	The Trojan Marching Band records its version of *Hit That,* the first single off The Offspring's long-awaited album *Splinter*, at Jim Henson Studios. Lead singer Dexter Holland supervises the recording session himself. The song is released that same year as a B-side track on the *Hit That* CD single.
OCT. 06	The Trojan Marching Band appears as itself on an episode of the NBC drama *Las Vegas*, marching through the fictional Montecito Casino.
DEC. 06	The band performs with KC and the Sunshine Band at halftime of the game vs. Oregon State at the Coliseum. The set includes *Boogie Shoes* and *(Shake, Shake, Shake) Shake Your Booty,* among others.
DEC. 13	The Trojan Marching Band opens for The Offspring at the Universal Amphitheater at the KROQ Almost Acoustic Christmas Concert. The marching band plays the rock band onstage with its rendition of *The Kids Aren't Alright*.
IN THE WORLD	The U.S. declares war on Iraq. Arnold Schwarzenegger is elected Governor of California. The Disney Concert Hall opens in Los Angeles. Dan Brown publishes *The Da Vinci Code*. *Finding Nemo* debuts at the box office.

2004

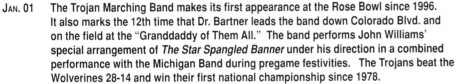

JAN. 01 The Trojan Marching Band makes its first appearance at the Rose Bowl since 1996. It also marks the 12th time that Dr. Bartner leads the band down Colorado Blvd. and on the field at the "Granddaddy of Them All." The band performs John Williams' special arrangement of *The Star Spangled Banner* under his direction in a combined performance with the Michigan Band during pregame festivities. The Trojans beat the Wolverines 28-14 and win their first national championship since 1978.

JAN. 22 The Trojan Marching Band returns to Hong Kong for its second consecutive Cathay Pacific International New Year's Parade, making the band the first American group to be invited to perform twice *(photo above right)*.

FEB. 08 The Trojan Marching Band backs up André 3000 of the hip hop megagroup *OutKast* for the finale of the 46th Grammy Awards at the Staples Center performing the #1 hit, *Hey Ya*.

MAY The band travels to Mainland China for the first time, visiting Beijing, Xi'an, and Shanghai. Highlights of the tour include playing *Conquest!* on the Great Wall of China and a reception at the ancient city gate of Xi'an, where Dr. Bartner is presented with the key to the city. The Trojan Marching Band also parades down a Beijing pedestrian mall as a pre-Olympic exercise for city officials.

APR. 13 The Trojan Marching Band – along with Sir James Galway, 100 flutists, and the Pink Panther – debuts the Henry Mancini postage stamp at L.A.'s Music Center for its first-day-of-issue dedication ceremony *(photo above left)*.

APR. 18 As part of the "Year of Mancini" celebration – honoring the 80th anniversary of composer Henry Mancini's birth – the band presents *Remembering Mancini* at the Cerritos Center for the Performing Arts. Mancini's daughter Monica and Plas Johnson – the original tenor saxophonist from *The Pink Panther* soundtrack – perform at the event.

FALL The band releases its 12th album, *the march to #1* and accompanying DVD of the same name. The CD contains live recordings of the band at the 2004 Rose Bowl, including the pregame, halftime, and postgame performances along with rock charts played in the stands during the action. The DVD is the band's first and features videos of the Trojan Marching Band's performances at the Rose Bowl plus footage of the band's rallies at Disneyland and Universal CityWalk.

OCT. 16 As a finale to the Trojan Marching Band's celebration of the "Year of Mancini," the band performs a Mancini halftime show at High School Band Day. Special guest star Monica Mancini performs *Moon River* with accompaniment by the TMB and massed bands.

NOV. 28 The Trojan Marching Band kicks-off the Hollywood Christmas Parade (again) in front of the Kodak Theatre on Hollywood Boulevard with *Hooray for Hollywood*.

IN THE WORLD President George W. Bush is reelected.
The 9/11 Commission report is released.
Athens hosts the Summer Olympics.
Martha Stewart is sentenced to five months in jail.
Lost debuts on ABC.

2005

HOPE · OPTIMISM · ENTERPRISE · FREEDOM

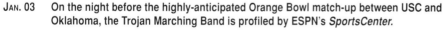

JAN. 03   On the night before the highly-anticipated Orange Bowl match-up between USC and Oklahoma, the Trojan Marching Band is profiled by ESPN's *SportsCenter*.

JAN. 04   The band appears at its first BCS National Championship game at Pro Player Stadium in Miami. It's the band's second trip to the Orange Bowl in three years. The band's condensed five minute pregame is considered by many Trojan fans to be its best ever. The Trojans destroy the Sooners 55-19 to complete an undefeated season. Many Trojan stars including Reggie Bush and Coach Pete Carroll lead the band with sword in hand for post-game renditions of *Conquest!*

JAN. 16   The Trojan Marching Band leads Joan and Melissa Rivers up the red carpet for the *Joan and Melissa: Live at the Golden Globes* pre-show at the awards ceremony.

APR. 10   The band's ninth concert in Cerritos is entitled *All That Jazz* and honors Dr. Bartner's 35 years as director. Special guests include Wayne Bergeron and Louie Bellson.

JUN   The Trojan Marching Band is invited to perform at World Expo 2005 in Aichi, Japan, its 4th visit to a World Exposition in less than 20 years. The band kicks off USA Day at the Expo, *(photo above)*, leading a parade from the U.S. Pavilion to the park's amphitheater. The band also visits Kyoto and Tokyo, performing at Tokyo DisneySea and at a Nippon Professional Baseball game. The Trojan Marching Band is the first American college marching band to perform at both venues.

JUL. 17   Dr. Bartner leads the All American College Band at the gala 50th Anniversary celebration for Disneyland featuring Julie Andrews and Governor Arnold Schwarzenegger.

AUG. 12   Dr. Bartner leads the All American College Band down Disneyland's Main Street for the last time after 28 summers at the helm.

SEP. 08   The Trojan Marching Band opens for Kanye West and Maroon 5 at the Los Angeles Memorial Coliseum for the nationally-televised *NFL Opening Kickoff 2005*.

OCT .05   David Conger, the Trojan Marching Band drum major, emerges from a birthday cake in front of Tommy Trojan with sword in hand as the climax of USC's 125th Anniversary celebration.

OCT. 15   The band celebrates with the team, Dr. Bartner pointing to Reggie Bush (5), in the endzone after the winning "Bush Push" touchdown as the top-ranked Trojans down the Fighting Irish at Notre Dame Stadium in what is considered one of the greatest college football games ever played. It's the band's 17th consecutive trip to the Midwest for the rivalry game *(photo above)*.

OCT. 29   Both George Lucas and Snoop Dogg visit the Trojan Marching Band at the Homecoming game versus Washington State.

NOV. 19   George Clinton and P-Funk perform *Give Up the Funk* with the Trojan Marching Band at halftime of the Fresno State game.

IN THE WORLD   Hurricane Katrina strikes Louisiana and Mississippi.
Two Supreme Court vacancies are filled by President Bush.
YouTube hits the Internet.
Brokeback Mountain debuts at box office.
Family Guy returns to FOX television after a three-year hiatus.

2006

JAN. 02   A steady rain for the full five and a half miles of the Rose Parade fails to spoil the Trojan Marching Band's 13th appearance during Dr. Bartner's tenure in that event.

JAN. 04   35.6 million viewers – the most for a Bowl Championship Series Game – watch the Trojan Marching Band's halftime performance at the Rose Bowl, including the debut of *Brooklyn* by Youngblood Brass Band.

MAR. 09   Dr. Bartner is honored as a Lowell Mason Fellow for his contributions to music education by the National Association for Music Education.

APR. 09   The 10th Pops in Cerritos concert titled *Celebration* is a special tribute to the Concert Band's first nine years at the Cerritos Center for the Performing Arts. It features artists who appeared with the band during this time. The master of ceremonies for the event is television legend Henry Winkler. Returning artists include Charlie Bisharat, Monica Mancini, and Barbara Morrison.

MAY   The Trojan Marching Band's 10th biennial international trip begins in Venice, then travels through Bologna on its way to Florence. In the Tuscan capital, the band performs a concert in the city's Piazza della Signoria in front of Michelangelo's David and in the nearby Boboli Gardens. The band then visits Rome, performing in the city's famed Piazza Navona, and leads a parade around the Colosseum.

SEP. 07   *Good Morning America* tapes the band forming the show's new "GMA" logo on Cromwell field. The segment is aired on the next morning's show.

SEP. 16   Ellen DeGeneres debuts her new DVD with the band's help on her television show.

OCT. 21   The Trojan Marching Band performs at the grand opening of USC's Galen Center.

NOV. 18   The TMB honors alternative metal band System of a Down at halftime of the Cal game. The band performs two songs from the group, then drummer John Dolmayan and guitarist Shavo Odadjian join in, performing on their hit *Toxicity* *(photo above)*.

DEC. 07   The Trojan Marching Band drumline and twirlers appear on an episode of the sitcom *Scrubs.*

DEC. 25   The band's drumline appears as the "12 Drummers Drumming" for the special *1 vs. 100* Christmas episode.

IN THE WORLD   Iran challenges the U.N. over enriched uranium production.
Democrats gain control of House and Senate.
Demonstrators protest nationwide against illegal immigration reform.
Pluto loses its status as a planet.
High School Musical debuts on Disney Channel.

2007

JAN. 01   For the 2nd year in the row, and the 14th time in 38 years, the Trojan Marching Band wows the crowd at halftime of the Rose Bowl with a set of modern hits: *Pump It* by the Black Eyed Peas, *Snakes on a Plane* by Cobra Starship, and *Toxicity* by System of a Down. The Trojans beat the Michigan Wolverines 32-18.

FEB. 14   The *Sports Illustrated* Swimsuit Issue hits the stands with a pictorial of Trojan Marching Band members in full uniform posed with models for the music-themed issue which claims a readership of over sixty million.

APR. 15   The 11th Pops in Cerritos concert titled *Strike Up the Band, The Music of George and Ira Gershwin.* Guest stars include jazz singer Patti Austin and pianist Shelly Berg.

JUN. 01   *The Sound of Victory* is the 13th Trojan Marching Band album under Dr. Bartner's direction. The CD features live recordings of songs the band debuted since Pete Carroll began coaching the USC team and the entire pregame show from the 2005 Orange Bowl. The album includes hits from System of a Down, Black Eyed Peas, Shakira, and Reel Big Fish.

JUL. 11   The Trojan Marching Band drumline is featured in the finale of the 2007 ESPY Awards at the Kodak Theatre in Hollywood. They perform Sly and the Family Stone's *Higher* with rappers Common and Macy Gray and guitarist Rocco DeLuca.

JUL. 24   ESPN flies a 10-Piece Trojan Marching Band unit out to its headquarters in Bristol, Connecticut to debut its daily *College Football* Live show with a sketch featuring host Rece Davis. The Trojan Marching Band participates in a "Battle of the Bands" opposite the Grambling State Band that makes *SportsCenter's* Top 10 Plays.

SEP. 19   The reality show *Last Comic Standing* Season 5 finale has the Trojan Marching Band performing.

OCT. 03   The Trojan Marching Band portrays a high school marching band on an episode of the sitcom *'Til Death.*

OCT. 06   The Trojan Marching Band marks its 250th consecutive football game attended, home or away at the Coliseum – USC vs. Stanford.

DEC. 09   A 10-Piece Trojan Marching Band unit travels to College Station, Texas to perform for the Women of Troy soccer team winning its first College Cup championship *(photo above).*

IN THE WORLD   Nancy Pelosi becomes the first female Speaker of the House.
The Subprime mortgage crisis hits economy.
Al Gore wins the Nobel Peace Prize.
The Mitchell Report exposes drug use in Major League Baseball.
The Last *Harry Potter* book debuts.

2008

Tuba player Ryan Suter meets *How I Met Your Mother* star, Alyson Hannigan, on the set of the show when band made a guest appearance for the episode *Three Days of Snow.* Hannigan, who received a People's Choice Award for best actress in a TV musical or comedy, described her experience with the band, "My absolute favorite [moment] is when the USC Marching Band played for me in the episode when Marshall and Lily are meeting each other at the airport," says Hannigan, who loves scenes exploring Marshall and Lily's relationship. "I was very pregnant, and even if I weren't pregnant, that was just such a touching moment. But to be hormonal, and to be serenaded with all of those beautiful musical people — I was bawling. And I wasn't the only one."

JAN. 01 For the fifteenth time, and marking the third year in a row, The Trojan Marching Band performs in the Rose Bowl debuting the Robert Randolph & The Family Band hit *Deliver Me* at halftime. The Trojans defeat the Illinois Illini, 49-17.

JAN. 11 The band's video recorded rendition of *The Pretender* by Foo Fighters – submitted in conjunction with YouTube's My Grammy Moment contest – is a hit, pulling in 64,000 views for the year – an auspicious launch of the band's own YouTube channel.

JAN. 25 The TMB joins special guest stars Oprah Winfrey, Jay Leno, and the Laker Girls for the taping of the 1,000th episode of *Dr. Phil.*

MAY In the Trojan Marching Band's first visit to South America, they perform concerts on the steps of Rio de Janeiro's city hall, on the famous Ipanema Beach, and at a Brazilian club soccer game. With this journey, Dr. Bartner has led the band on six of the world's seven continents, excluding only Antarctica.

MAY. 21 Some 31.7 million viewers in the United States see the Trojan Marching Band on the Season 7 Finale of *American Idol* at the Nokia Theater in Los Angeles.

OCT. 16 The band helps the landmark Philippe's restaurant in Los Angeles celebrate its 100th Anniversary by entertaining the thousands of patrons waiting in line for 10 cent French Dip sandwiches.

OCT. 16 The Trojan Marching Band performs for the highly-anticipated world premiere of *High School Musical 3* at the Galen Center.

DEC. 11 In an episode of the CBS sitcom *How I Met Your Mother,* the Trojan Marching Band portrays the fictional Arizona Tech Fighting Hens Marching Band.

IN THE WORLD Sarah Palin is announced as the Republican vice presidential candidate.
Oil prices soar during the summer.
Michael Phelps wins a record eight gold medals at the Beijing Olympics.
The New England Patriots' perfect season is ruined in the Super Bowl.
The Dark Knight becomes one of the highest-grossing films of all-time

Dr. Bartner welcomes Matt Leinart, one of the most famous quarterbacks in USC history, to the Rose Bowl game in 2008. Leinart played in the 2003–2005 seasons.

2009

Jan. 01   Dr. Bartner leads the Trojan Marching Band for his 16th Tournament of Roses, marching in the Rose Parade for the fourth consecutive year. The halftime show includes *Almost Easy* by Southern California metal band Avenged Sevenfold. The Trojans beat Penn State 38-24 *(photo right)*.

Feb .08   The band performs for the second time in five years on the Grammy Awards. This time they collaborate with legendary British alternative rock group Radiohead making its first appearance on the show. Their live rendition of *15 Step* is one of the most acclaimed performances of the night.

Feb. 22   Two weeks after its appearance on the Grammys, the Trojan Marching Band continues its run of the awards shows as the drumline collaborates with Hugh Jackman, Beyoncé Knowles, and the stars of *High School Musical* and *Mamma Mia!* for the 81st Annual Academy Awards at the Kodak Theatre. For this third appearance on the Oscars, the drummers – in full tuxes and top hats – back up the all-star cast in a Baz Luhrmann-produced salute to the Hollywood musical.

Apr. 01   On a prerecorded promotional segment for April Fools Day, the Trojan Marching Band surprises Hugh Laurie and the cast of *House* by bursting unannounced into a scene they are filming.

Apr. 06   The band opens the first *SportsCenter* broadcast from Los Angeles at L.A. Live, backing up hosts Stuart Scott and Neil Everett with the show's trademark theme.

Apr. 23   The band debuts its own Twitter account to communicate with fans and friends.

Jun. 17   The Laker Band is part of the Lakers Championship parade from Staples Center down Figueroa Blvd. to the Coliseum. Band members ride atop a fire engine and play *Fight On!* as they pass the USC Campus.

Jun. 18   At a morning ceremony, the Trojan Marching Band reopens Universal Studios' backlot at the famous Courthouse Square. Staff members from *The Tonight Show with Conan O'Brien* hear the band and invite the Trojans to come on the show that night, becoming the first marching band to appear on the show, which had just debuted on June 1.

Sep. 14   The TMB performs at the L.A. Dodgers' "USC Day." Before the game, the band performs the National Anthem and Dr. Bartner – wearing a special number "40" jersey – throws out the first pitch. The band also performs *God Bless America* on live television during the 7th inning stretch.

Sep. 29   In what is billed as the "most elaborate" Macy's Stars of Dance segment ever on ABC's *Dancing with the Stars,* the TMB marches into the studio, performing *Get Down Tonight.* The band is accompanied by dancers co-choreographed by Chuck Maldonado (of *Stomp the Yard* fame).

Nov. 14   The TMB releases the 14th album (and fifth CD) of Dr. Bartner's tenure. In honor of his 40th season, *Trojan Legacy* is a special double CD album, mixing new recordings of hits from the Pete Carroll era with original renditions of classics from the first 13 albums. Included in the 40 tracks is a special rehearsal recording of *15 Step* with Radiohead that Thom Yorke gives his special permission to include.

Nov. 26   The TMB appears on a special Thanksgiving episode of *The Jay Leno Show.*

Dec. 05   For the last game of the season, the band WAR joins the TMB at halftime, performing their hits *Low Rider, Cisco Kid*, and *Why Can't We Be Friends.* Comedian George Lopez guest conducts the band for the performance. The Offspring's Dexter Holland is also honored by the TMB at the half. Before the game, L.A. City Council members present Dr. Bartner a resolution in celebration of his 40th season.

Dec. 26   The TMB makes a daytrip to San Francisco to cheer the football team on to a 24-13 victory over Boston College in the Emerald Bowl. The rainy game is Pete Carroll's last as head coach of the Trojans.

In the World   Barack Obama becomes the first African American President.
The Swine Flu outbreak ignites fear of a global pandemic.

A Tribute to Dr. Arthur C. Bartner
Professor of Music
University of Southern California
and
Director of the
USC Trojan Marching Band

by

Brad Calhoun

The Voice of Troy

1983-1988

So how does a skinny trumpet playing kid, born and raised in New Jersey transform the University of Southern California's Trojan Marching Band into the *Greatest Marching Band in the Universe*? Let's count the ways:

First - Dr. Bartner has a deeply felt and profound passion for excellence.

Second - He has an unparalleled work ethic for over forty years. Just ask his beautiful wife, Barbara, and his two wonderful and now adult children, Steven and Debbie, about the hours, days, and months they sacrificed to Dad's "USC Band family."

Third - How about Art's raw talent that empowers him to lead band performances that send shivers down the spine, and can move audiences to tears when they hear his renditions of the *National Anthem, Fight On, Conquest, Tribute,* or the *Alma Mater*.

Fourth - Perhaps, it's because the USC Trojan Marching Band is known throughout the world from their platinum records, numerous motion picture and television appearances, performances at the Hollywood Bowl, and even the opening of the 1984 Olympics with Aaron Copland's *Fanfare for the Common Man.*

Fifth - And his own countless awards and guest conducting on the national stage.

Sixth - Add to all these things, his absolutely undying enthusiasm for each new football season, or the new band camp when the freshmen learn the ropes.

Seventh - And a renewed thrill each time the band marches triumphantly down the peristyle stairs of the Los Angeles Memorial Coliseum to the thunderous approval of some ninety thousand Trojan family members.

Let's be clear about this: Dr. Bartner's life's work continues to produce what all Trojans know to be true. He more than anyone in the history of USC has shaped, honed, and defined *The Spirit of Troy* that courses through the veins of every Trojan.

Many people would be satisfied with this legacy, even embarrassed to be acknowledged in such high and lofty terms. But as great and true as these accolades are, they are only partial truths about Dr. Arthur C. Bartner. That's the essential problem with the biographical genre — words cannot adequately convey the full meaning.

There are literally thousands of former students, band members, staff, colleagues, friends and family whose stories of how Art has touched their lives represent myriad pieces in this mosaic of his legacy. My story is just one that reveals a deeper truth that points to the essence of Art's contribution as an educator that I want to share with you.

I first became aware of Dr. Arthur C. Bartner during the fall of 1972, a year in which the USC football team won the National Championship. I was dating a freshman co-ed who would become my wife. She was a music major enrolled in Dr. Bartner's spring beginning winds class, where she learned to play the tuba. Funny stories abound, but after graduation, they became fond memories of a valued professor.

In 1980, life's journey brought me to USC as a development officer for the then School of Performing Arts (Cinema, Music, Theatre). From my office at the north end of Bovard, I could often hear the band practicing on Cromwell Field.

One day, I couldn't resist the opportunity to go out, sit in the stands, and watch the master-teacher at work. Microphone in hand, perched atop his ever-present ladder, he screamed instructions—sometimes vein-popping directions to a wayward drummer, sloppy clarinetist, forgetful trumpeter, or confused flag girl. Nothing escaped his perfectionist eyes.

"Band, ten-hut, ten-hut, USC!" echoed over the campus on practice days until dark. I so loved watching the transformation from utter chaos on day one of band practice to the precision performances at half-time on game day—watching Art "do his thing."

One day as I was watching, Art seemed to be coming toward me. My first thought was, "Am I doing something wrong? Is he going to yell at me?" You can imagine my shock when instead he said very calmly, "I notice you've been coming out to hear practice for a number of weeks. Do you think the trombones are on the beat?"

I was completely blown away (no pun intended). Art Bartner was asking me, a complete stranger, what I thought of his band's trombones. And he continued, "I want to know what you really think. Don't hold back."

That first fateful conversation led to many more. Eventually we enjoyed collegial lunches on campus, then our families met and shared meals. My wife was able to re-connect with her former tuba professor. By the time three years passed, it was 1983 and Brian Heimerl, who had been the Voice of Troy since Art began at USC was ready to move on. Art asked if I would become the new Voice of Troy. I jumped at the opportunity.

My story reveals the truth about Dr. Bartner's genius—and I don't use that word lightly. The essence of his genius is when he is a catalyst unlocking the talents or capabilities of another—encouraging and motivating another, whether it be me, or any of his thousands of students over the years. Art is then, in the truest sense of the word, an artist who unlocks the deepest truth and gifts inside others so that they in turn, share their artistry with the world.

So to my dear friend, Art, thank you. Thank you for giving us everything you have to give so that we can all be better.

Fight On!

In Appreciation

For Photo Scanning

Fabian Corona   Allen Eckhouse   Pavel Gordeyev   Niral Patel   Ryan Suter

For Additional Research

Rob Hallam

For Additional Assistance

USC Bookstore – Mark Ewalt, Dan Archer & Dan Stimmler

Wright Color Graphics – Linda & Mike Fullerton

USC Sports Information Department – Tim Tessalone & Paul Goldberg

University Archives – Claude Zachary

USC Football – Ben Malcolmson

Friends & Members of the Trojan Marching Band

Elizabeth Geli, Richard Escobedo, T. J. Breisacher, Vicki Tisdale, Steve Bloom, Alan Kita,
Lesley Ruzon, Justin Wilburn, Craig Elliott, Deborah Thompson, Troy Wollwage, Dawn Kita,
Michael Vazzana, Danielle Martinez, Monique Ramirez, Cynthia Wiese, Gretchen Meier,
Kellie Graham, Brian Padelford, Dan Schwartz, Woody Kane,
Gretchen Heffler, Mel Keefer, Barry Spanier

And Special Thanks

To all Trojan Marching Band Members who, through their spirit, devotion, and sweat, have
created The Greatest Marching Band in the History of the Universe

Index

Photo Credits

ABC Broadcasting Company	68
Academy of Motion Picture Arts & Sciences	28
Benjamin Chua	18, 49, 73, 203 (left), 204 (bottom)
Brett Padelford	10-11, 14-15, 16, 42, 46, 48 (top), 65, 70, 74, 84-85, 115 (top) 117, 118-119, 128-129, 146-147, 154-155, 158 (bottom left), 159 (top right), 159 (center right), 161 (bottom), 180-181, 201 (left), 201 (right), 203 (right), 205, 206-207
Brian Padelford	89
Courtesy of Craig Caldwell	168 (top)
Courtesy of James F. Ward	179 (top)
Dan Avila	17, 43, 44
Dan Avila/Ruben Davila	130-131, 132, 133, 134, 135 (top), 135 (bottom), 136 (top), 136 (bottom), 137, 138, 139, 140 (all), 141 (all), 142 (all), 143 (all), 144 (bottom), 145 (all)
Dr. Bartner Personal Collection	80, 81 (top), 81 (bottom), 122-123 (all), 162 (bottom), 166, 170, 178 (right), 189 (left), 189 (right), 190 (right)
Fox Television	69
Fran Operchuck	90-91, 92, 93, 94, 95, 111
Jeff Kravitz/FilmMagic	26
John Soo Hoo/Los Angeles Dodgers	162 (top)
Michael Yada/AMPAS	30
Morris Finkelstein	159 (bottom left)
Peter Read Miller/USC Sports Information	156 (top)
Robert Jensen	5
Roseanne Keefer	51 (left), 51 (right), 60, 159 (bottom right)
Ruben Davila	120-121, 156 (bottom), 168 (bottom left), 176 (bottom left), 176 (bottom right), 199 (top)
Selby Shlosberg	204 (top)
The Tournament of Roses Archive	72-73
University Archives	182 (left)
USC Sports Information Department	86, 167 (right)
Walt Disney Company	45
Warner Bros. Records	24
West Coast Aerial Photography	19

All other photos from Trojan Marching Band Archives

The Man on the Ladder

by

Keith H. Walker and Robert W. Jensen

Published by

FIGUEROA PRESS
840 Childs Way, 3rd Floor
Los Angeles, CA 90089
Phone: (213) 743-4800
Fax: (213) 743-4804
www.figueroapress.com

Figueroa Press is a division of the USC University Bookstore
Copyright © 2010 all rights reserved